Five Children,
Five Cases,
Five Pounds

Brigid Patricia Boggan

Note for Librarians: A cataloguing record for this book is available from Library and
Archives Canada at www.collectionscanada.ca/amicus/index-e.html
ISBN 1-4120-7779-6

*Printed in Victoria, BC, Canada. Printed on paper with minimum 30% recycled fibre.
Trafford's print shop runs on "green energy" from solar, wind and other environmentally-
friendly power sources.*

TRAFFORD
PUBLISHING™

Offices in Canada, USA, Ireland and UK
This book was published *on-demand* in cooperation with Trafford Publishing.
On-demand publishing is a unique process and service of making a book available for
retail sale to the public taking advantage of on-demand manufacturing and Internet
marketing. On-demand publishing includes promotions, retail sales, manufacturing,
order fulfilment, accounting and collecting royalties on behalf of the author.

Book sales for North America and international:
Trafford Publishing, 6E–2333 Government St.,
Victoria, BC V8T 4P4 CANADA
phone 250 383 6864 (toll-free 1 888 232 4444)
fax 250 383 6804; email to orders@trafford.com
Book sales in Europe:
Trafford Publishing (UK) Limited, 9 Park End Street, 2nd Floor
Oxford, UK OX1 1HH UNITED KINGDOM
phone 44 (0)1865 722 113 (local rate 0845 230 9601)
facsimile 44 (0)1865 722 868; info.uk@trafford.com
Order online at:
trafford.com/05-2676

10 9 8 7 6 5 4

I dedicate this book to my family and cousins who encouraged me to write my life story. It is eventful, sad and sometimes funny. It began 8th April 1925, in a pretty historical town, on the south east coast of Ireland.

VERY SPECIAL THANKS

I wish to thank my cousin Paul for his encouragement, his lovely wife Clair for the typing; without her help it would have been impossible for me to write this book. To my friend Mo, for her interest and enthusiasm. For the medical team both in Ireland and England, who advised me to get it all down on paper, believing that expression was the best cure for depression; I am not however convinced of that theory.

This book is meant to be a simple explanation of my life and the times I lived in. A story of how I coped with situations and hardships, decisions that had to be taken for my children, when I just hoped and prayed the decisions I was taking were the right ones for their future. Survival was the priority. I followed my motherly instincts - it was my best effort.

I started the book in 1987 but abandoned it more than once, finding it too painful and difficult to write about. Then deciding I owed it to my children, relatives and friends, and so many nice people that crossed my path during my life, so with all the courage I could muster I took up the pen once more and began the journey again. Now I am glad I told my story. It's social history. Times are so different now. I am hoping the reader finds my book interesting.

I would also like to thank my son Billy for designing the cover.

Chapter 1

MY CHILDHOOD - GROWING UP - MARRIAGE
Full of laughter, full of love, full of tears

A WOMAN'S JOURNEY

I WAS BORN IN MY GRANDMOTHER'S HOUSE in 1925, much as I am told, to everyone's delight, being the first grandchild. The place was a small seaport town on the south east coast of Ireland. It was very hilly and quaint, with lots of history, and surrounded by several beautiful seaside resorts and historical buildings.

In those days class distinction was very prevalent in Ireland. My mother was born in to a wealthy family. She had high school education and was at boarding school until she was eighteen.

My father was a native of a neighbouring town, and held a rank in the Irish army when he and my mother met; she was then 19 and he was 21. Mother's family never really accepted him as they felt he did not come up to their standards. My father was a very intelligent man and the jobs he held were mostly clerical. But he drank a lot and this problem was to last through his entire life.

My mother, because of the sheltered secure life and upbringing, wasn't coping well with family life, and she seemed to be always trying to escape. The friends she was with at school were now mostly married to professional men: dentists, solicitors, that sort of circle, and she would constantly get away afternoons and evenings to visit them and it always seemed hours before she came home.

✵

I was the eldest of 14 children, 11 girls and 3 boys. I spent a lot of time in my grandmother's house and I loved being there. It held a sort of magic for me, and food was always being prepared and cakes were baked. My aunt also had a large family, two girls and nine boys.

By about 1923 mother's family business was on the decline and most of them lost almost everything. My grandfather died at the age of 49 so my mother's family were struggling. The house was still there; my aunt and grandmother took in boarders. So there was my aunt's family, my uncle, my grandmother and me, popping in and out all the time.

The old house had nice furniture, good cutlery with their initials stamped on them, nice silver ware and linen table cloths etcetera, so I suppose you would say it was a grand old house, in complete contrast to our own corporation house on an estate, two bedrooms, small hall, parlour, living room sparsely furnished with gas lights. It was a cold bleak house with concrete floors no covering on the stairs, straw mattresses made with coarse sacks, a range to cook on, a sink in the corner of the living room for washing. We also had a big tin bath for bathing us children; the cleanest child got in first the dirtiest last.

I was taught by nuns, good teachers they were, kind they were not, at least not to deprived children anyway, but I suppose they were women of their time and did what they felt was right, poor consolation for the victims. I was in what was called A Stream all the way through school and my best subjects were English, Irish, religious knowledge and drama.

I struggled a lot due to an inferiority complex. Little wonder when you were asked first thing on a Monday morning if you had the money for your books in front of a class full of girls and you had to say, "Sorry, no," or you had a darn in your sock and not allowed to sit in the front row with the better dressed girls, most of them in uniform, and I was a very sensitive girl.

I hated Mondays because on that day you were expected to have the money for your books, and I rarely had it…

We had candlelight often as there was no money for gas. Or maybe the gas mantle was broken and there was no money to replace it. The candle was carried around on a saucer. Cups were without handles. Jam jars often replaced the cups and we always put a spoon in before we poured the tea so it wouldn't crack. Bedclothes were scarce so coats were useful to keep us warm and I remember newspapers on the back windows at night, as we had no curtains.

Mammy nearly always managed to get out in the evenings, visiting her better off relations, probably to unburden her problems and chat. Being aged 12, I would have rounded the younger children up from playing in the street.

After I had helped daddy to get the baby settled, I would sit with the younger ones around the turf fire. I remember very severe winters and the concrete floors added to the coldness of the house. Daddy would sometimes have to break up a chair and make the turf last.

So we sat on the floor in the candlelight and the glow of the fire with our coats under us to feel comfy, and told ghost stories. Mine were usually very dramatic, to get their attention. They would be about the banshee who appeared after midnight, combing her long hair and moaning. This was usually a sign in Irish folk lore that someone was going to die, especially if it was a dark, wild night.

The little ones would listen and watch me intently, and I would really enjoy getting their attention. Daddy would usually be reading the paper, borrowed from our neighbour, until he thought I was going over the top then I would be told very quickly that it was nine o'clock and bed time.

❋

It was on one such night we were all settled in bed. Daddy, strictly in charge of course would shout up the stairs, "No noise now, say your prayers and straight to bed!" I was second in charge and would often have to get in and out of bed to separate the younger ones who were fighting, until I could finally settle with my magazine, with the youngest one sleeping in the crook of my arm.

One night, the candlelight was burning low on the saucer and it was a strain to read my love story. I dropped off to sleep with Siobhan, aged 14 months, in my arms as usual. I awoke to find she was missing. I ran into daddy's room shouting and crying, "Daddy, Siobhan is gone!" Daddy was in bed reading a book and mammy was still out. He looked at me with alarm saying, "What the hell are you talking about? How could she be gone?! Jumping out of the bed and chasing after me, we both searched frantically around the room. We discovered Siobhan under the bed – sleeping and very cold.

I can recall the fear and I shrank back from daddy, expecting to get a wallop. Instead, shaking his hand at me in anger as he discovered my magazine where it had dropped out of my hand as I fell asleep, he said, "Now, young lady, get down on your knees and pray this child hasn't caught cold, because you will have your mother to deal with and only God can help you then!" I was relieved, yet frightened at the same time. I did get down on my knees and prayed, "Please, dear God, don't let Siobhan die!"

Getting back into bed with the baby, I listened intently to her breathing and cuddled her to warm her cold little body. I heard mammy come in and could hear daddy and her talking. When she came into the room, I pretended to be asleep.

She tapped me on the shoulder saying, "Now you can get into your own bed and I'll deal with you in the morning." I thought to myself I couldn't have luck talking about the banshee and hoping it wasn't Siobhan that was going to die, or maybe even myself.

❋

When I was 14, I was sent to the dispensary to collect our monthly free milk tickets, it was a very cold morning and my head and throat ached. When I got back home the doctor was called. I had diphtheria. Everything in the house had to be fumigated and it must have been embarrassing for my parents with such primitive bedding and mattresses. Throat swabs were taken. I was sent straight to hospital where I couldn't believe I was receiving so much attention.

It was a fever hospital and I had a lovely bed with nurses fussing around me and nice food served on a tray. I was praying my third swab would be positive after six weeks you could not be discharged unless your last three swabs were negative and so I hoped maybe I would get paralysis as this sometimes happened after diphtheria, and I would be kept in then. But I recovered and left the fever hospital after six weeks.

Everyone was pleased to see me back home, but soon all was back to normal I was minding the children and running the messages again as usual.

It was mostly cast off clothes we wore, given by mammy's friends, most of them were married and did well financially, so we looked forward to these parcels of clothing, as they were new to us.

Daddy lost many jobs because of his drink problem and this caused unpleasant rows in the house which frightened me. If he had been working and got home late, mammy would be asking for the money and there would be an ugly scene. I would be praying that daddy would fall asleep in the chair or go to bed before anything happened.

It was very sad I thought, daddy had this problem, because he was such a nice, kind man really and mostly well thought of by people. He enjoyed making our meals, putting the babies to bed, sterilizing the bottles and teats and there was a new baby nearly every year, but he loved all the babies.

※

Mammy did not seem to have the patience daddy had with us, maybe being thrown into all the poverty from her secure background, she couldn't handle it, yet she could be funny and had a good sense of humour – quite a complicated character really. Her friends loved to meet her and she told witty stories and made them laugh. She was known for her hats and wouldn't go out without a hat even though her shoes were shabby and down at heel.

She loved to go to the pictures and enjoyed being out meeting people; being tied in looking after children wasn't her thing at all and she knew we were in good hands with daddy, he loved the home.

Late at night daddy would be sitting repairing our shoes and polishing them specially for Mass on Sunday. I remember they were heavy lace up shoes, hard wearing.

※

My little brother died as a baby, I would be about 12 years old then, and I remember seeing him in the bed in the parlour, he had just died. Daddy said, "Go down to your grandmother and see if your mammy is there. Tell her to come home quickly, Michael has died." He was only 8 months old and mammy had gone to the dispensary to get a prescription for him, and would usually call in on my grandmother before coming back. I ran to find her and she was there and came back with me.

I also had a sister, Mary, who died in daddy's arms when she was only 2 months old. It was in the front bedroom up-stairs, which had a small grate and took less coal than the range. Daddy was sitting on a chair with the baby in his arms. I don't recall the funerals at all...

My sister Margaret, died in hospital at 14, from Meningitis. I do remember that funeral, and being in a car with mammy; she was very sad and crying a lot. Daddy was heartbroken over Margaret's death and went to her grave every Sunday on his bike, taking his trowel to tidy and weed it.

He then said he had a dream about her – she stood at the end of his bed and he asked her if she was happy and she said, "Daddy, you don't know how happy I am." He was crying as he related this to me.

Daddy did go to England a few times as we got older, to find work. But he never stayed away more than 12 months at a time; he loved home and I think he missed the family life. While he was in England money was sent regularly and he always had money when he came home.

In those days babies were christened within a week of birth, and registered. Also women were 'churched', meaning you were received back in to the church after the birth of a baby. You held a lighted candle and the Priest said prayers over you.

It was believed that babies born with a membrane covering their head and face were born with a caul and they were considered lucky. The membrane was dried by the midwife by being spread out and looked like a fine veil. Sailors liked to carry some with them as an assurance they would never drown. Some of my own sisters were born with the caul. I remember neighbours calling at the house and mammy handing the envelope containing a piece of this precious caul.

It was all home deliveries in the '30s and castor oil was a common lubricant that women used when they felt they were going into labour. I recall mammy always having a small bottle of castor oil and she would squeeze an orange into a cup and pour the whole bottle of castor oil into the orange juice and drink it quickly.

Maybe an hour or so later the midwife would arrive with her little clutch bag and go straight upstairs to mammy.

Daddy would have kettles and saucepans of water boiling on the range for the nurse. Soon we would have another baby. I often wondered what the newspaper parcel contained that the nurse would hand to daddy; he would lift the kettle, shove it well into the fire and then replace the heavy kettle. I later realized it was the afterbirth.

Then us children would all go upstairs and see mammy with the new baby. Mammy would get a nice hot cup of tea, and the room smelled strongly of disinfectant and baby powder.

Chef sauce bottles were used to feed the babies, instead of the usual boat-shaped type. The teats had deep rubber bands that slit easily after constant use. Having no money to replace the teats, I would hold the prepared bottle of milk, cocoa, or sweet boiled water tightly between my knees and bandage the teat securely around the bottle top and knot it tightly to prevent it leaking.

Another invention was to put a cork into one of these deep rubber banded teats, which acted as a dummy and prevented air getting through and filling the baby with wind. Some of my sisters sucked these up to 3 years of age.

If there was no cork available the teat gave off a whistling sound from different directions of the room, depending upon whichever bed the babies slept in. I remember mammy once remarking she felt like a bird fancier, but it did the trick of soothing the child to sleep.

Some of our beds had no mattresses, so it would be common to get coarse sacks from the factory – they would be rejects. Mammy would fill them with straw and sew them together. I recall getting an oily smell from the sack. The straw made a solid base to lie on. The younger children would wet the beds constantly, which meant the sacks had to eventually be burnt in the back garden and replaced.

As the years slipped by we got a little better off, what with daddy getting the odd job and some of the older children going to work. We progressed onto better beds, often sleeping four to a double bed, heads and tails – two to the top and two to the bottom. A bucket was placed on the landing for our convenience.

That's just the way life was at that period of time in Ireland; the 1930's were rough.

❈

At about the age of 7, I developed a bad stammer and would not go out on any errand without a note and would even cry if I didn't have a note written to explain what I wanted. I would keep repeating, "I can't say it." This continued for several years and at school when geography, history and spelling questions were asked; it was so frustrating, I knew all the answers but the words just wouldn't come.

But I managed to stay in 'A' Stream through the school years. Eventually the stammer eased, yet I cannot recall what stage of my life I overcame it, or why it should leave me.

I remained anxious through my whole life, fighting hard not to let it get me down. Perhaps the reason I was affected so badly by the circumstances at home was being the eldest, so much was always expected from me.

As a child and teenager, I loved Christmas, although there were no presents or new clothes, but I recall that it was a wonderful atmosphere. Around the town the greetings of "Happy Christmas!" to neighbours and everyone you met, then "Many Happy Returns" seemed to go on for weeks before Christmas arrived. Then visiting the crib, and seeing turkeys hanging – feathers and all in the butcher shops - and wishing we could have one of these in our house for Christmas.

Plucking the turkey was a big operation and there was a technique to this. Apparently you plucked the feathers out in one direction, just as they lay on the bird. In many houses the old fashioned ovens weren't big enough to hold the bird and in this event the turkey was prepared and stuffed, and placed in the roasting tin ready to be taken to a confectioners in the town that opened up early Christmas morning specially, so that people could avail themselves of the service of having the turkey cooked.

❈

It also had to be collected, so it was not uncommon to meet people, especially women, at 3 or 4 o'clock on Christmas Day, carrying the precious bird, covered with sheets of newspapers, to their homes.

The plum puddings were boiled for 8 hours, in large cast iron pots and watched carefully in case the pot boiled dry. Water was added from a kettle kept boiling nearby and you smelled the aroma all over the house - all adding to that special time of year, Christmas.

We had lots of snow and ice, weather was more predictable in those days, with hard winters. I loved to see the snow and ice but hated when the girls and boys threw snowballs, aiming for your neck so it melted down under the collar of your coat.

The day after Christmas we called St. Stephen's Day. It was customary to see groups of children gathered outside the houses singing, "The wren, the wren, king of all birds," and end with "We wish you all a Happy New Year with plenty of money and barrels of beer."

They kept up the singing until the door was opened and they got their reward, which might be only a penny or half penny. They had bunches of holly and ivy, waving it to the tune they sang. More often than not snow would be falling and most of them were covered in snow, with red noses. I took my little cousins on that day to visit the crib in the churches, weather permitting. We then went around the town for a walk.

The better off children would be out in their cosy new outfits, a lot of them sporting white fur on their collars and pushing prams with dolls, or with scooters or bikes.

My auntie dressed me for my Holy Communion and had a cap of pearls made for me by a lady that made hats on Browns Road; it hugged my head, fitting snugly over the veil. That was in 1932. It was unusual and greatly admired when mammy took me visiting all my cousins. Some of them kissed me and said I was like an angel, others asked me to pray for them. They all gave me money.

❄

Grandmother and auntie thought I was beautiful and I had to stand for them and then keep turning around. It was a wonderful day.

Aged about 7, I remember grandmother making me a big rag doll, starting it in October for Christmas. It was fascinating to watch this doll take shape, equally to notice the folds of flesh that seemed to droop from grandmother's neck just under her chin. I couldn't resist examining it or caressing it as she worked away on the doll. I would ask her why her neck was all loose like that. She would smile and say, "Because I'm getting old," and I would get weepy saying, "You won't die will you?' Amused, she would reply, "No, not yet love," giving me a reassuring hug.

That rag doll was as big as myself. It had a flat face with eyes, nose and mouth drawn perfectly on the face, at least I thought so. Examining it carefully, the arms and legs dangled. I would hold it tight to see if it really was as big as me. I carried it everywhere with me, even to bed. I didn't take it home as all my sisters would want to hold it and I was very possessive about that doll.

My auntie started preparing for Christmas always in September, that magical time of year and very interesting for me. I loved to kneel up on the chair watching her mix the Christmas cake and puddings, beating eggs, sifting flour and sugar. She had a bottle of Guinness and whisky nearby. The pudding was prepared and a large fine cotton cloth was dipped in hot water, greased and floured and prepared pudding mixture placed in the centre of the cloth, which was then gathered carefully and tied with string or twine, leaving a little space for the pudding to swell while cooking in a big oval-shaped pot, already on the stove with water bubbling.

An enamel plate was laid on the bottom of the pot, to prevent the pudding cloth sticking. The precious pudding was lowered gently into the pot, tightly covered, and bubbled away on a low heat for 8 hours, boiling water added from time to time to make sure it didn't boil dry.

❋

On completion it was removed and allowed to cool, before hanging it from a butcher's hook from the pantry ceiling - where it matured until Christmas Eve.

The boys would thump this with their fists, and the aroma of spices and alcohol filled the house, giving a lovely festive homely atmosphere. The Christmas cakes were wrapped in greaseproof paper and stored in the recess of a long red wardrobe that had gold leaves scattered all over it. This was in Auntie's bedroom. Occasionally I would open the doors, to get the smell of Christmas.

Anticipating it delighted me, this time of year there was so much to look forward to. Everyone seemed to be happy, especially when asked, "What are you getting for Christmas?"

Although I did not have any illusions about Santa, I liked to believe in him. When you are the eldest of 14 you get wise very quickly, especially when you listen to your parents getting anxious as Christmas approaches.

Hearing them discuss how many pairs of shoes and warm coats were needed, I grew up very quickly. A gypsy once told me I would be old when I was young, and be young when I was old, and I think I found that to be true. Those were eventful years with hard work, and strict schooling; nuns were great teachers and took no nonsense.

A huge turkey, feathers and all, would be delivered to my grandmother's house a couple of days before Christmas. This had to be plucked then cleaned out, and wiped clean. It hung from the ceiling in the pantry until the festive day arrived.

Potato stuffing was then prepared - cooked potatoes mashed with butter, seasoning, finely chopped onion and mixed herbs. The bird was stuffed at both ends with this mixture. Auntie used a needle and cotton to draw the flesh together, preventing the stuffing escaping. This was usually done on Christmas Eve when it was covered with a large tea towel and allowed to rest until early next morning.

❅

Then it was placed in a huge roasting tin, surrounded with fat from the turkey that was saved from around the neck area of the bird.

Butter was rubbed into the skin and it was placed in the oven, carefully checking the time. It took 6-7 hours and rested for one hour before serving. When the oven door closed, I thought, 'Imagine, I have to wait another whole year to experience this again!' Thinking, 'I hope I won't die before it happens'.

I was allowed to stay in grandmother's house at Christmastime as I was one less to take care of at home, with so many mouths to feed. It was a busy Christmas Eve with my Auntie getting all the presents out for my little cousins. Most of the lodgers had gone home for Christmas.

The parlour was a very big room, the fire place being the main feature. Old fashioned black and white marble it was - the blazing fire of coal and turf created the atmosphere. It blazed away, especially when the lights were switched off, and the flames danced around the walls that winter's day.

Being taught how to set a table at a very young age. I was in my element given these jobs. The large table would be prepared with the best linen tablecloth and serviettes, wine glasses which you only saw in the Christmas season, accompanied by the water glasses and jug. Then came mixed pickles with so many different shapes in the jar. Next, the canteen of cutlery was taken from the sideboard drawer, doilies and serviettes, and the three tiered cake plates with a lace doily placed on each cake stand.

Some of my relatives would arrive on their way back from Mass on Christmas morning and were greeted warmly and given a glass of sherry and a slice of Christmas pudding. Before partaking of this though they would take three sips of cold water from a glass after receiving the sacred host, (in the name of the Father, Son and Holy Spirit) The carols we sang added to the joy of the day.

Carol singers stood in groups in the street singing *Silent Night* and they were all muffled up with suitable clothes, covered in snow.

There seemed to be a hush about at Christmas-time, except when the pubs closed and some loud singing was heard on the streets, usually Bing's song, **White Christmas**. My Grandmother would dryly remark, "Listen to those blackguards going home to their poor wives". I enjoyed all of it and I was so happy with my rag doll.

Dinner time finally arrived. Turkey was placed on the white scrubbed kitchen table where a large meat platter awaited its arrival. Stuffing scraped from the bird was transferred to a serving dish and the special dinner service placed to warm in the oven. The sherry trifle looked so delicious in a big glass dish, topped with lots of cream and cherries, accompanied by a dish of jelly.

There was always a red Christmas candle placed close to the window, in remembrance of the birth of our Lord, and to light Mary's way to Bethlehem. The decorations around the house were usually hand-made and secured with brass drawing pins, which were stuck in the ceiling for weeks after Christmas.

I always remember the crib, with beautiful life size figures, arranged in the centre recess of the big wardrobe that seemed to take up the full length of the wall in Auntie's bedroom.

My uncle set up the lighting to shine down on the infant Jesus. On the twelfth day the Wise Men were placed at the back of the crib with their gifts and were fascinating to watch at night, again with the lights in the room switched off.

Grandmother and Auntie were always glad to get a rest from the children, when I took them out to see the church cribs in town.

❈

Getting back home to all the festival goodies, again making the most of all the rich food still being produced on the table and nice Christmas songs on the radio; I liked to wallow in it all. My rag doll was propped up in the big arm chair, with a blanket wrapped around her to keep her warm. I stuck her under grandmother's bed when it was time for me to go home to my own house, and hoped she would be safe until I came back.

When I arrived home I would boast to my sisters about all the nice things I had for Christmas. Mammy and daddy always appeared anxious and worried and it was such a different atmosphere at grandmother's.

I loved drama and was good at it in school. I also loved Irish step dancing, but there was no money to pay for any kind of music lessons. I felt cheated that I couldn't learn so I had to suppress those big ideas.

I felt frustrated especially as the eldest of a large family for there was little enthusiasm from my parents, who were wondering where the next meal was coming from. The '30s meant survival.

I was a very emotional child and cried easily. My father once remarking, "Brigid's bladder is very near her eyes," and that upset me even more because I was really sad and no one knew.

When daddy was lucky enough to get a job on the grant, mammy would send me to a nice shop that sold country butter and crusty bread and small seed buns. One penny these buns cost and they were hot and would keep your hands warm on a cold day. Porridge oats and yellow meal were to be seen in sacks outside grocery shops and you could buy sixpence worth of vinegar if you had your own bottle.

Crubeens, (pigs trotters) were a great treat at three pence but were sticky to eat. Butchers shops sold you one shilling's worth of stewing beef and a marrow bone for soup.

❊

Most of the butchers had sawdust strewn on the floor, and white scrubbed counters, cleaned with a wire brush. Pigs' heads that were pickled, and sheeps' heads also were easily available and made good meals for large families.

We always had coal clubs, and the Jew man for clothes. You could pay 5 shillings or 2 shillings weekly high interest that you were not always told about, but that didn't worry you too much as long as you got the new coat or dress.

Woolworths was a great store and everything in the shop was sixpence. Lipsticks were in small tubes, when you reached the end you scooped it out with a match stick until it was absolutely empty. There was tinted velouty cream, Ponds products were also available, and we used Vaseline for eyelashes and eyelids. Blowing the lighted match out, you drew the ash part across your eyebrows. Lux soap and Cutacura talc was available - if you were lucky enough to have the money to buy it.

There was also a soap called Dirt Shifter, dark in colour, powerful and cheap. Iodine was the common disinfectant for grazes and cuts, but it stung.

If there was a nit infestation at school mammy saturated our hair in paraffin oil, using a fine comb. We would be lined up in the kitchen for this treatment on a Friday or Saturday night. We were vaccinated against TB and diphtheria, both dreaded diseases.

Virol was seen in a lot of houses as a pick-me-up for children. If you were run down, Guinness was recommended. Egg flip was another tonic (egg and milk whipped). Camphorated oil was used for chest infections and then a warm flannel applied and you stayed in bed until your body had absorbed all the oil.

We sometimes flattened bottle tops which we called 'teetees' and to do this we would use a hammer, being careful not to get it too much out of shape, as it was to go in the gas meter when we didn't have a penny.

❋

When the meter was eventually emptied by the collector lots of teetees would tumble out. Mammy would remark, "It must be one of the children who did that now". Avoiding the rent man was a common occurrence, we would all have to be quiet while he continued to knock, and wait until he was well out of the street before we emerged.

Daddy made pancakes, with flour and water. They looked lovely but were too tough to get your teeth into. Fried bread was a common meal in the morning. My cousin who lived near us saved bacon rasher fat for us in a cup. We could keep the cup, delighted that it had a handle. Shaking salt on fried bread made us thirsty for lots of tea.

I was domesticated, if only in my mind, at the age of 15. I would be thinking, 'Now if I were mammy, when I got the dole money on Fridays, I would buy ½ stone flour and 4 pence worth of buttermilk to bake lots of bread and just line up all the baked bread on the table, and some of the bread would be brown, made with wholemeal and soda.

I'd have a big turf fire blazing (cheaper than coal), mashed potatoes with chopped onion, and porridge for breakfast with fried bread and lots of toast and margarine, although I hated the strong taste of margarine. All sounded so easy to dream about. Putting it into practice was another thing. Still, I could dream.

Daddy grew lettuce in our back garden, along with cabbage, spring onions, beetroot and carrots. At one time he had a plot and could sow potatoes. He would have us children shovelling horse manure in buckets from the street, as most house deliveries then were by horse and cart. Sheeps' heads made good soup, with onion and barley. Pigs' heads were a common Sunday lunch, with cabbage. Half a head would cost 1 shilling and, sixpence, according to size. Daddy used lots of mustard with that meal and had some of the meat cold for his tea in the evening.

❄

Mammy never liked these kind of meals. Her childhood was so protected and money was plentiful and there was a maid to do the housework. She wasn't coping with the poverty, and a husband with a drink problem. She must have despaired at times.

Daddy was a very clever man and neighbours would knock on our door and ask if daddy would write a letter for them, especially if it was an important letter applying for a job or writing to the government about something or other, and he would always oblige.

We had a picture of the Sacred Heart in our kitchen that had a little red bulb light in front of it, which never went out. It was a wedding present my parents had received from a relative and one day during the great poverty, one of my sisters stood in front of that picture and said, "You are a very cruel God!" – but at least she believed in Him.

Times were very tough and I remember actually having porridge for my dinner one Christmas day. That particular year daddy went to England to find work and it was shortly before Christmas that he left.

I was taken out of school at 15 and sent to work in one of the local factories. Mammy knew somebody in the management so my age was covered up, as I was supposed to be 16. It was about a 3 mile walk to work and back again. Wages were just 30 shillings weekly, but it was exciting, I was now working and growing up.

Passing my grandmother's house on my way to work I often called in and had a bowl of porridge, as there might be no breakfast at home, at least not most mornings. It was a

6:30 a.m. start from home as I clocked in for 8 a.m. and I was walking, hoping eventually to get a bike.

Taking some lunch with me as work didn't finish until 5:30 p.m. It was an 8 hour day and if there was overtime it could be 10 hours.

❊

My lunch often consisted of just dry bread, sometimes I did have a cheese or meat sandwich, but those were on good days. Some days I just had dry bread wrapped up which I kept on my lap during lunch hour and nibbled it out of sight of all my working companions, all of whom seemed to have nice brown soda bread and meat sandwiches. Most of the girls were farmers' daughters.

It was in the factory that I met my best friend, Mary. She was pretty and very adventurous. We worked together on the sausage loft with lots of other boys and girls, linking sausages and tying up black puddings and luncheon meat. I suppose there would be at least twenty of us around a big table weighing off and linking the sausages. We chatted and sang along as we worked and generally had a good old laugh except when the foreman and the manager were around.

We worked very hard in a very cold environment and at the end of the day it was boots and rubber aprons on and scrub down the huge floor of the sausage loft. All the left over sausages and black & white puddings were carried by us girls in to a very big freezer to be stored. The lads attended to the sides of pork or beef joints. Often I remember being in the freezer, which had big heavy doors, and one of the lads would wait his chance and follow me in, closing the door and doing his best to get a kiss. I would be lashing out and screaming, and the charge hand might open the door shouting, "What the hell is going on in here?'" and the poor lad was caught red faced.

The factory was in the countryside, surrounded by big green fields. In 1941 the war was on and we had practice air raids, just in case of attack. The whistle would sound once for all the workers to stop work, take off the white coats and hats we wore and run towards the fields. I would say that there were as many men as women, so the race would begin and the lads had a great time chasing the girls across the fields.

We all had to lie down for the mock air raid, until the whistle sounded. Twice meant 'all clear' and we all had to return. That was a job for management as the workers were making the most of the opportunity and the language from the management left a lot to be desired, however we were all eventually back at our jobs.

By this time I was working 12 months and got a new Raleigh bike for 2 shillings sixpence a week. Daddy always checked the brakes and kept it in top condition. I handed my pay packet in at home and got back 7 shillings, and 2 shillings 6 pence had to go to pay for my bike.

There were platform dances and middle-pieces on then in the country and we could cycle to those. Usually it was piano accordion music, great fun. It would be summertime so we had the moonlight to light our way home. Mary and myself would cycle home, and maybe a few more of the girls with us, singing as we went along, after a great night dancing.

The ballroom dances were held at the weekends in the town, with the big band sounds. These sometimes went on until the early hours of the morning, except during Lent. For those 7 weeks there was no dancing, beginning again on Easter Sunday.

We acquired a radio – great excitement. The radio brought a great deal of entertainment into our homes in the 40's and 50's – *The Waltons, The Riordans* – and during the war we had Lord Haw Haw on the news. And Victor Sylvester's music was magic.

My friend Mary suggested to me one Monday at work that it might be a good idea to run away. It sounded exciting and I asked, "Where to?" and she said, "England." We could stow away on the boat, otherwise we would need passports. We discussed it while we were linking the sausages.

Mary was one of four, her father worked at the factory so they were fairly comfortable. I always envied her nice dresses and her granny always made a fuss of her. Because I was the eldest of such a big family and my father unemployed so the more I considered running away the more attractive it became. So our plans began in earnest.

We threw little hints here and there to our workmates that we might one day end up in England, but they really didn't take much notice of us. However payday Friday arrived. Our pay was now £2– 10 shillings a week. Mary and myself collected our wages and cycled for home.

Calling at my grandmother's and told her the machines at work had broken down. I collected some clothes I had at my grandmother's and told her I was taking them home for washing.

It was a small parcel. Mary continued on home. We made final arrangements to meet on Croke Road at 2 o'clock with whatever clothes we could manage to take without attracting too much attention to ourselves.

First of all I had to get rid of my bike, so I called on a lady I knew on Park Street and asked if I could please leave my bike with her until I was passing back, and she agreed. I pushed it out into her back yard and thanked her, and went on my way to meet Mary. She was there on the dot.

Mary wasn't pleased I was carrying a parcel as she had put all her clothes on her. We now decided to call at the bus office on the Quay, where we handed in the parcel until we checked in for the Dublin bus, leaving at 5 p.m. We then proceeded to Woolworths and purchased tooth paste, a tooth brush and face cloth.

Mary was chatting away, imagining us having the sky for a roof, and peeling potatoes for the crew on the boat. We both had vivid imaginations. However we now had two hours to spare so we decided to go to the pictures. Ginger Rogers was starring in *White Collar Girl* and she was running away in the film. Mary whispered in my ear, "Get a few tips from her!"

We had to keep checking the time from the clock in the cinema, in case we missed the Dublin bus and we actually had to leave before the film was over. Making our way to the bus office to collect my parcel, as we got close to the office I noticed to my horror, my aunt was walking up and down outside with a garda.

I grabbed Mary's arm and said, "Oh my God, what will we do now?" She in turn got hold of my arm, pulled me into a hardware shop (Harveys) which was next door to Grogan's and told me to keep watch.

As soon as my aunt turned her back we ran out and up a side street onto O'Connell Street and over a bridge.

We had by now missed the bus; it was coming on for 5:30 p.m. and all the workers were beginning to leave the factory to make for home. By this time we were nearly to a country road, where there were ditches either side, so we decided to climb over the ditch in case we were seen by any of our working companions, as most of them went along this road on their bikes.

We were the topic of conversation and quite clearly we could hear some of their remarks, of course listening intently, and it went like this, "What will become of those two young girls at all, I wonder if they are in the family way, and if their jobs are gone. Night is drawing on now, God help their fathers and mothers."

We were both crouched behind the ditch, feeling a bit hungry and scared, I was anyway. As soon as we felt the last few workers had gone we emerged. The next bus due was the Cahir bus and we didn't have to wait long until it arrived.

Mary had an aunt living in Cahir as it happened so she informed me we could go to her for the night as she always knew Mary wanted to go to England.

She was convinced her aunt would help us to get to Dublin and stowaway from there. By this time I was feeling sick, as I wasn't a great traveller, thus adding to Mary's problems. She told me, "You can't get sick now as we are nearly there." Putting out our arms, we stopped the bus and got on.

Thankfully it was only about a two hour journey. We finally arrived in Cahir. Mary's aunt lived down a little laneway, off a side street. When she opened the door and saw Mary, she put her hands up to her mouth and said, "My God Mary, what are you doing here at this hour at night?"

Mary tried to pacify her, saying, "Now I always told you I wanted to go to England, and promise you won't tell on us. Brigid and myself will leave here in the morning for Dublin and are going to stowaway on a boat from there."

I was still feeling sick after the bus journey and when her aunt said, "Would you like to go to bed now, or to the pictures?"

I was dying to go to bed, but Mary decided we would go to the pictures. Her aunt said, "I must go out now and get milk and eggs for the morning. I'll be back soon." What we didn't realise was that she had gone to phone the garda barracks .

She returned with her shopping and took us to the pictures, where we were soon eating sweets and watching the film. After about an hour and a half through the film, the usherette was shining her torch on us to say Mary's father was at the entrance with a taxi waiting to take us home. But Mary didn't give in that easily, she shouted at the aunt for telling on us and urged me to run through all the seats and try to get out of the exit.

By this time I had enough, so we both went to the entrance, to face the music. Mary's father was delighted to see her safe and well.

I was petrified on the journey home, thinking about facing my mother, father and aunt. The taxi eventually pulled up outside my grandmother's door. My aunt and uncle were standing on the pathway outside the house. My aunt had her arms folded across her chest, raging mad at me through the car window, "How dare you do this to your mother? She is down in the Garda Barracks, waiting for news of you."

My uncle was standing behind her, smiling and winking at me, and saying, "Never mind, it will be something for you to remember later on. Now, sure all is well. They are safe and back home, thank God. They will both be back in work tomorrow." But I was now really feeling sick, and knew the worst was yet to come.

We arrived at my house and Mary's father walked me to our front door. My heart was pounding. Daddy opened the door and ordered me up the stairs immediately, to await the return of mammy. I didn't dare let myself imagine what the confrontation was going to be like.

On parting with Mary, the arrangements were made that she and myself would meet at the usual place next morning and go to work together, after praying in the nearby church, as we usually did.

In the meantime I ran upstairs and my sister Margaret, aged 12 years, was standing at the top of the stairs. She was upset for me and kept saying, "Why did you do it? My mammy is going to kill you." So I suggested she got into bed, which was a single bed, and I got in behind her, keeping my coat and beret on, which was straight on my head. I had long dark hair that I rolled in a coil all around the beret, Vivian Leigh style, although I really thought I was like Barbara Stanwyck, but at that moment I was past caring what I looked like, wishing I could die. Hearing voices downstairs, I knew mammy had arrived.

She tore up the stairs and the next thing I knew I was being pulled out of the bed by my hair and my beret went flying. I hit the wall and she was screaming at me, "Why did you do it? Is there something wrong with you?"

I did not realise at the time she meant, was I pregnant? I said, "I don't know." She said, "You don't know?" Jesus in heaven. What am I going to do?"

If the woman only knew I did not know how you got pregnant. I had heard the whispers around the factory, which I thought were pretty disgusting anyway. Mary's explanation was not very enlightening, "Be careful how a boy kisses you as you might have a baby." So I was always careful about that. Mammy's advice was, "Hold the bone and the dog will follow you. Give it to him and he will run away with it." So I was totally confused!

After collecting my bike, Mary and myself met as arranged next morning, meeting up with our work mates also making the journey to the factory. Of course they gathered around us to hear all the news and what we had been up to. It was a bit outrageous to say the least for two girls to run away in 1941. They expressed their surprise at the nerve we had coming back to work.

We had to give an account of ourselves to the manager, and that didn't make us feel any better, although Mary was a bit of a 'devil may care' and just shrugged it off, as if to say 'why worry'?

We both clocked in, leaving our bikes in the bicycle shed as usual. As we passed through the different departments to be interviewed by the manager and foreman, we had to pass the departments the lads worked in. They were clapping their hands, stamping their feet and doing all they could to embarrass us. However, coming face to face with our employers was a very serious business. The meeting was short. We were suspended for six weeks.

The manager informed us, "Arranging passports takes a long time, so you had better take that time off." I just said to myself, "Sacred Heart of Jesus, I place all my trust in you." So we both calmly walked out, heads down, through the same areas, management following close behind us.

No commotion this time. Just dead silence. We clocked out and collected our bikes. Mary, optimistic as ever remarked, "Never mind, we will call into the church again and say a prayer, and we could still get the 10 a.m. train to Dublin!"

Even I was surprised at this suggestion after all we had been through, but I firmly declined and said, "Oh no Mary, this time I just have to go home." With knees shaking and heart racing at the reaction of my parents, amazed at how calm Mary was, I was wishing I could be like her.

I kept thinking about daddy not working and my job gone as I handed over my pay packet. That wage would be a big loss at home and there'd be no money to pay for my bike. All this kept going over and over in my head.

Mary kept going on about a great dance that was coming on Wednesday night and the popular band. I was friendly with one boy that played in this band, he had walked me home from the dance a few times. Mary also had a boyfriend. We kept wondering how we would face them again.

We parted at the end of our road and I made my way home. When I got in daddy was shaving and looking in a little mirror on the wall in the kitchen facing the door, and he said to mammy, "Jesus, Mary and Joseph, the young brat has been sent home." Mammy looked at me as If I'd crawled out from under a stone.

After a long lecture I was locked in the parlour, which had a single bed in it, so I had plenty of time to think. One of my sisters brought me a cup of tea and toast during the day, saying, "I've been told I must not speak to you and I have to lock the door again when I go out."

I was allowed out of the parlour again on Tuesday and mammy was going to see the management in the factory to ask for my job back and explain the hardship it was causing.

I was kept in so I knew I couldn't mention the dance on Friday night, but I decided I would steal out of the parlour window at 7 o'clock and go over to Mary's.

So off I went and called at Mary's house. She was sitting on a chair in the kitchen with her feet in a basin and her granny had another basin, washing Mary's neck. Her mother was ironing her dress, green taffeta, in preparation for the dance.

I thought Mary was like a queen and thought, why couldn't things be like that for me? I could not help but wonder why she would want to run away from all that comfort. Her mother said I could have a wash in the sink.

Mary lent me a pale blue chiffon dress and a little blue bow for my hair. I had long dark hair and secretly I thought I looked nicer than Mary that night.

My shoes were a bit shabby but at that moment I just lived for the night and was excited about the dance. Off we went to the ballroom, reaching the door, and hearing the music was like magic.

I was then in my own little world of make-believe. I was told so often how pretty I was, I felt good about myself, at least for a little while. Then my friend who was playing the drums caught sight of us both, and the band struck up *Home, Sweet Home Again, No More Roaming.*

We soon attracted a crowd around us, wanting to hear all about our adventure. My friend came over to me during the interval and said he was never so glad to see anyone in his life, as he had been seen taking me home a few times and it had been rumoured that I must be pregnant. The poor lad.

I was watching the clock to leave and get home by 10:30 p.m. I put the bow from my hair in my pocket and my coat covered the dress. I hated leaving the dance. I got home about 10:30 and sure enough, daddy was at the door, waiting for me. I got another lecture for sneaking out like I did, but I thought it was worth it.

Later I was lying in bed, going over all the happenings of the night. The Fortys being a very romantic time: big band sounds, sentimental songs, slow waltzes, tangos and rumbas. I was just in a different world and the hours flew by. I was popular and hardly ever sat out a dance. Our local band always closed the dance with the tune **Who's Taking You Home Tonight?** and the way they asked to take you home was "Would you like to get your coat?"

And you always had a good idea who it would be, as he booked you for many dances during the night, especially the last one.

The morning finally arrived with the news that I could return to work, but not Mary. I was shocked by this and insisted I couldn't go back without Mary, it wasn't fair. But I could not win that one. My parents were very indignant about my attitude saying, "You'll do as you're told and go to work. The money is needed here and your bike has to be paid for. Mary's father is working, yours is not." That finished my friendship with Mary. She was not taken back for six weeks.

I reported for work that morning and had a good talking to from the foreman. I felt I had two heads walking in, especially without Mary. It was embarrassing explaining to all the other girls the circumstances, but I was soon accepted back and things were back to normal. But I felt embarrassed for a long time and missed Mary's friendship a lot. She refused to speak to me and it was to be many years later before we spoke again.

FIRST DATE

It was shortly after this I met Andy, while passing through the slaughtering department at work. There was an iron staircase that led onto the sausage area where I worked and the girls got a lot of wolf whistles from the lads. We enjoyed the attention. A lot of the girls were more outgoing than I was, and secretly I thought it was vulgar and common to whistle. Andy worked quite close to the staircase, oil skin apron tied around his waist and knee length Wellingtons pulled over his trousers. His cousin worked beside him. They looked very attractive in a rugged sort of way, and very charming.

Andy began to send messages to me and waited at the gate at closing time, in order to chat me up. I declined for a long time – for a few weeks at least. It certainly wasn't love at first sight. Something deep down was saying to me 'no'.

I had noticed him previously at the local dance hall, being an observer. I felt he was a bit of a flirt and I liked seriousness, I was of course flattered by the attention and he wasn't to be put off.

Our first date was for the pictures. He bought sweets from the kiosk on the way in and went to the ticket office, I assumed for two gallery tickets, so I walked in the direction of the stairs, but he tipped my arm and directed me to the door of the cheaper seats 1 shilling 3p as opposed to 2 shillings for the more classy ones - a big let down.

I was amazed at his cheek but then I looked down at the bag of sweets in his hand and thought, 'Sure God love him, he did think of the sweets.' A few times during the show I stole a look at his side face and noticed his nose was very long, but his hair was nice and wavy. I tried to get a look at his hands to see if his nails were clean but I couldn't see them in the darkness.

He was neat in his dress. I wore a light navy travel coat, which I had purchased from the Jew man for 2 shillings a week. I had long hair coiled up over the ears and loose over my shoulders and it bounced when I walked so I felt glamorous.

I was then 17 and everything was exciting; the dimly lit streets as the crowds emerged from the cinema and walking up hilly Thomas Street where you got the smell of fish and chips coming from the chip shop. Even the rain if it fell was pleasant, and when it was frosty it glistened on the pavements and the moon shone and there were lights in shop windows, this was my little magic world and it was free.

My dates continued, but they had to be far away from my own house and that of my grandmothers; but word soon got around that I was walking out with a boy regularly - a big commotion. Being the first to grow up is hard and I was headstrong, that's how my father described me. He was right, because that determination was to see me through life.

My sister Lena followed me out at night when she would skip along behind me chanting, "Mammy told me to watch you!" She caught me one night linking him and ran home to report the incident, that was serious stuff in 1942.

The first six weeks of our courtship was very timid. We walked out in the country and sat on a wall. I made sure there was about two feet between us. By this time I liked him but it was six weeks before he ventured to kiss me good night, at the top of the street where we lived, and I remember running home and getting quickly into my little bed to think about it, and I cried myself to sleep. You could say I was over emotional and I thought, 'That's it now, there is no going back after that.'

Mammy was impressing on me that she was arranging for me to go to England with Lena to work in a convent in Middlesex, and arranging passports, which were in force then due to the war between Germany and England. And I was to put marriage out of my head, if that is what I was thinking about, because that was not going to happen!

Lena was then 15 years old and excited about going to England to work. After Lena there was Margaret, Una, Vera , Nancy, Jimmy, Maura, Niamh and Shiobhan. Mary, Rita, and Michael had died in infancy.

My passport actually came through. I was discussing all this with Andy and he was telling me he would throw himself under the train I was on, and that impressed me. I thought, 'Imagine how much he loved me, to think about doing that.' Of course it was the topic of conversation at my grandmother's.

Word had also got out around the factory that I might be getting married. By this time I had met all of Andy's family; he had two sisters, and a brother married with a few nieces and nephews. His mother was a kindly hard-working woman, and it was obvious that she spoiled all her sons, especially Andy.

During all this debating Andy knocked at my grandmother's house one day and announced who he was. My aunt thought he was an insurance man but her tone lowered when she heard his name. She called my grandmother who softened a bit when she saw him, and invited him into the parlour.

He said to her, "Please Mrs. Phelan, will you try and influence Brigid's mother against sending her to England, and I promise you," getting down on his knees and showing her his two hands, "while I have these she will never want for anything!"

❄

She related all this back to me later and said although she was quite firm in her objecting to the relationship as I was far too young to even consider having a steady boyfriend never mind marriage, she did have sympathy for him. I'm sure they were amused as well as being very concerned in case I really was thinking about marriage.

My head was in a spin by this time, I could go to England with Lena or I could marry Andy, who by now was proposing with all his heart and painting pictures of our life together. We would have our own flat and fireplace, nice table and chairs. I would be knitting on one side of the fire and he would be sitting at the other side reading, and we would go for walks or to the pictures, but above all we would be together.

His mother told me he was walking the floor all night talking about me going away, so I promised him I would not go to England and that we would think of something. We often called to see his sister.

On one visit she said she would come with me to buy a suit for my wedding, and that we could buy the ring in the local pawn shop.

His sister was married herself and had two children. She suggested we had the wedding breakfast at her house and tell my mother I was going to a party, (My father was working in England at the time.) and that after the party I would be staying at Andy's sister's overnight. She and her older brother would be maid of honour and best man.

So Andy and myself called down to the Presbytery to see the Priest and we saw the canon, quite a strict abrupt man, and unfolded our story to him of how my mother and father would not consent to the marriage. I was surprised to notice how confident Andy was when talking to the canon; I on the other hand was very nervous.

Anyway the canon agreed with my parents that we were indeed too young to consider marriage.

❋

During our discussion it was becoming obvious the Priest was not impressed with Andy, and Andy said, "If you don't marry us, I'll take her to England, and marry her in a registry office."

That did it. You didn't talk to the clergy in Ireland like that in 1943. He ordered Andy out saying, "How dare you speak to me like that?!"

He beckoned me to stay behind for a little while and he faced me across the table, seriously saying, "I don't like this boy, or his attitude, but if you insist on this marriage I will have to go to the Bishop and discuss it with him, as its more than likely you will end up having to be married anyway."

Arrangements were then made for us to go back and see him in 7 days. We went the following week. He had seen the Bishop; permission to marry us was granted. Plans began in earnest for us to marry in the parish church before the 7 a.m. mass. In March 1943 I was 18, Andy was 21.

Chapter 2

OUR WEDDING TOOK PLACE AS ARRANGED: I wore a check brown/beige suit and a full veil pillbox hat. The breakfast was held at Andy's sister's house, as planned. An old grandaunt of mine, saw me getting married before mass that morning and called to tell mammy on her way home. Mammy fainted and eventually sent a wire to my father working in England and informed him of the marriage.

On the way back from the church I sat on Andy's knee in the front of the car next to the driver, Molly and Bob in the back and whoever else could climb in.

I remember turning the wedding ring on my finger and repeating over and over again in my mind, ' I'm married, I'm married.' It just would not sink in.

It was so early in the morning that not too many people were around to see us slip into the house and we ate away at the breakfast table, listening to the piano accordion and had a big sing song and there was dancing when the table was pushed back. But all the time my mind would drift to my mother and father, and the dilemma they would be in, and last but not least my lovely grandmother and auntie.

As I was imagining the commotion, I had spasms of absolute terror, because they all had had such high hopes for me. I was considered pretty and intelligent, and class distinction being what it was those days, they had hoped some professional man would come along one day and ask me to marry him.

I struggled to keep my attention on the wedding group and appear normal. Andy's brother's wife Nan volunteered to go over and tell my mother the news. Andy seemed to be having a certain amount of gratification as he remarked, "They couldn't do a thing about it now I've married you."

※

The honeymoon was spent at his sister's - one of the loneliest nights of my life. Andy was in a drunken state in bed, and I was kneeling on an old leather armchair in the bedroom that had horsehair sticking up through it and it was rough under my knees.

I was crying, looking out the window and trying to get a glimpse of my own house, which was barely in view, as it was a big estate. I felt very sad at the hurt this would cause my parents and the disapproval it would meet with in my grandmother's house.

From then on it was sink or swim. I could not be seen for three days after being married, as it just wasn't done for the bride to be seen in public. Andy was out every night with his friends, and I sat in with his sister.

He changed almost immediately and continued to live as though he was a single man. A week after being married he took me to the pictures. My mother sent word to tell me she didn't want to see me. I was then living very much with his people. I was soon to discover I was pregnant.

MARRIED LIFE BEGAN

We moved from his sister's to a room in the city centre at Mrs. Mac's. We rented a room at the top of her three storey house which was furnished: a bed, table and chairs, small fire with grate, and cupboard for food. I came down three flights of stairs in the morning where I had the use of the kitchen to cook breakfast on her electric stove.

During the early part of my pregnancy I caught scabies. I broke out in a rash all over my body. One morning I made my way to a nearby chemist just a few doors down the road. The chemist thought I had scarlet fever and called the doctor for me, who diagnosed scabies.

✳

He said I just took the weight of them from someone I sat next to, as they were highly contagious. So it was hot baths and medication. Baths were a tin bath on the floor of the room, the water boiled in saucepans on the grate and I always waited until Andy went out.

I wrapped myself in an old blue silk bedspread and slept at the end of the bed, not to have any contact with Andy, in case he caught it. He showed no interest and certainly no compassion. They were long, lonely days. Mrs. Mac was kind and often knocked on my door to see how I was, but because scabies were contagious, she couldn't come in and do anything for me. Eventually I got better and nobody caught them from me. I washed and boiled all bedclothes to eradicate any re-occurrence.

Following this I was about 6 months pregnant and I went down stairs at 6.30 one morning to get breakfast as usual. I came up the stairs carrying a tray with teapot, egg and porridge and slipped and fell on the stairs. Andy stood looking at me, swore and said, "That's my 'so and so' breakfast." He climbed over me and left for work.

Mrs. Mac came out of her bedroom and helped me up. Andy came home from work that evening and never asked me if I was hurt, he just showed annoyance and dead silence. A few days later I had a threatened miscarriage.

By this time I had made friends again with my mother and grandmother and auntie. Of course nothing surprised them about Andy and they would just say, "Well what did you expect?" Unhelpful, but there was no answer to that.

So I went home to mammy, with bad stomach pains and a slight blood loss. She got me to bed and called the doctor, and I was ordered bed rest for a week. I stayed with mammy and the doctor called to the house twice that week to see me. After the week was up I went back to our room.

❋

During the following week, while I was still taking things a bit easy, Andy's mother came down. It was a Friday fast day, and she cooked eggs and chips for him, and set the table. I had a premonition of what was going to happen when he got home as he liked good meals and freshly cooked.

He took the plate of egg and chips, and scraped them into the back of the fire grate, remarking, 'I wouldn't eat that s—," and of course I should not be sick either, but on my feet looking after him. When his mother called later that evening and I told her, she was not surprised at all but would still make excuses for him and say, "Sure, maybe he was in a bad mood."

I went into premature labour on Friday night 17th December 1943. I walked over to the hospital - which was about a quarter of a mile away. Andy had gone out as usual but Mrs. Mac walked with me and my little case. I was admitted but discharged again on Sunday morning the 19th as it was very slow labour. Andy's mother gave me 6 Beecham pills, which were very strong laxatives. I was in agony all Sunday night, not knowing if it was bowel or labour pains I had. Andy was sleeping away in bed, I just could not wake him.

About 6 a.m. in the morning I made my way down to Mrs. Mac's bedroom and called her, and she immediately went to wake Andy. He wasn't too pleased at all at being woken up to this, and it was snowing to add to his annoyance. He pulled on his trousers and shoes and he almost ran me through the snow to hospital. That was Monday December 20th 1943.

The baby was a breach birth, feet first, and it was 2:30 p.m. before the doctor could turn the baby. I had a forceps delivery at 5:30 that evening. A little boy, premature, weighed in at 6 lbs, and I had eight stitches. The baby was covered in cotton wool, and a little bonnet.

❋

The doctor came back to check him out next morning and told me he was premature and a little weak but he should be okay. He was a beautiful baby.

Andy wouldn't stay too long on his visits and they weren't every evening. That embarrassed me, as the other patients' husbands stayed until the bell rang for visitors to leave, which made me feel so sad and let down. Now we had a baby, and still his attitude was the same, but when you're 18, you're optimistic and hopeful. I suppose I thought that maybe he would change and when I was home with the baby, things would be different. I was dreaming of getting a pram and dressing it up with a nice frilly pillow, and my friends meeting me in town and I could show him off.

I wasn't good at sewing, but I was planning to learn to knit the baby's clothes. The arrangement was that we would live at Andy's mother's house for awhile, until we found a bigger room for the baby. The nurses were concerned as I was young, and they were instructing me on management. Because he was premature they said only the mother should handle the baby for a few months. I asked them to tell my husband this, as I knew his mother had old fashioned ideas about babies, and she might be taking over and doing things her way.

I knew Andy was resenting being told this and remarked to me it was a lot of rubbish, so I was worried before I left hospital. Confinement time in hospital was then 10 days. His mother's house, in a back lane off a main street, was one of 7 houses; 4 on one side, and 3 on the other.

It was a narrow white washed lane, with the houses quite close together, and a little latch on the outside of the front door that you pressed with your thumb to open. You walked in to a fairly big room that had two small windows, one to the front and one looking on to the yard.

※

Two bedrooms led off the front room, with a small window in each room. An attic staircase faced the back door and a fairly big attic bedroom. There was a hob fireplace to cook on. This had a small oven that you lit a fire under a tiny door that closed and kept in the fuel.

There was a flat iron bar that went across the main fire which was quite large, and this conveniently held saucepans, kettles and frying pans. The chimney was large so you had to be careful when cooking to secure lids as smoke or soot got into your cooking and frying was a problem. There were two cupboards, one had a mirror top old-fashioned sideboard effect. These held the Delph, crockery, and a dish on top to hold your eggs.

There was a scrubbed table and 4 chairs. Coal and turf and sticks were kept in a cupboard under the stairs and a small door with a little bolt concealed these. A wardrobe stood in one room and chest of drawers in the other. A big

yard at the back, with an outside toilet, and a tap on the wall
with running water, and a long clothes line. His mother, his
sister and her husband and two children, also lived in the
house. We had the attic bedroom and the stairs leading up
to it had a narrow ladder effect. It was a bleak room, with a
small skylight, a double bed, bare floor boards, and a small
wooden chair.

MY FIRST BABY

I bought a small pram second-hand from a lady in Dalton
Road, that included a pram cover which was fluffy and
I thought it was pretty. I remember dying that cover a few
times just to make it look different. You bought a dye then
for 2 pence. Luckily the top could be lifted off this pram and
taken upstairs for the baby to sleep in, on the floor by the side
of the bed.

We settled in this house. Andy's mother was a good woman and hard working. It was evident she spoiled her children,
especially her sons and liked to control everything. As far
as this woman was concerned, I would know nothing about
bringing up a baby, so no notice was taken about what the
hospital said. Given half a chance I was in fact very capable,
and had taken care of my own sisters and cousins from a very
young age.

So the lovely little baby was handled by everyone, and I
didn't have any say in that. That was painful as I was posses-

sive about my baby and very concerned that the advice from the hospital was being ignored. But I had to live there, at least for a while, as there was nowhere else to go. I coped best I could with that situation and the baby, whom we called Noel, was thriving slowly.

I was careful to attend the clinic regularly to have him weighed and assessed. His grandmother loved Noel, of course I had no doubt about that, and I am sure without meaning to she was just taking over. But my first baby was so precious to me, I wanted him all to myself, and he was a frail baby and needed careful feeding and nursing.

The baby hadn't brought Andy and myself any closer together and conversation was even more difficult now there was a house full of people, With him more or less on his own ground I was at a disadvantage in his mothers house, just cooking for him, and generally taking care of him.

One thing I was not to forget was Andy's pushbike.

On advice from his mother to continue to do as she did, as his mood was not good in the morning, I pushed it outside early in the morning under the window. Then he wheeled it through the house and outside into the yard in the evening when he came from work.

His lunch was packed and put into the bag on the back of the bike. He liked to be called an hour early, to give him time to wake up. Then it was pot luck what mood he would be in.

Breakfast finished, he then had easy access to his bike, and I breathed a sigh of relief if all went quietly, and another morning was over. Because usually getting the fire started to prepare his breakfast was always a pain. There was an old tin blower which was supported to keep it in place for a draught, though if the sticks or turf were damp it was hard to start. You were down on your knees blowing it into a flame, or fanning it with stiff cardboard.

His mother was as anxious as I was that everything was ready for Andy in time, or else all hell broke loose in that house, everything was, for peace sake! If the egg was not cooked to his liking he would tip it onto the floor, any back chat from me and I was pushed against the wall. It would more or less be my fault for not timing the egg properly, his mother remarking, "Sure you must know by now what he is like."

Then there would always be an atmosphere when he returned from work in the evening at 6:30 p.m. Madge's husband left for work later in the morning about 8:30 a.m. so I was out of the way while she prepared his breakfast. I envied her, Bob was a bit loud, but so easy going and so kind hearted. The evening time was always a problem, especially if Madge was going out with Bob the same time as Andy.

There were two small enamel basins, one laid on the chair in the kitchen and one in the bedroom, so they each could have a wash and Madge's husband took his turn to use the basin in the bedroom.

The flat iron was placed in the fire and you spat on it to test the heat for your ironing. There were loose collars attached to shirts by little buttons, and these had to be starched. Andy's appearance was very important to him, including a good sharp pleat in his trousers; this was another of my important jobs.

All washing in those days was done by hand in a big tin bath balanced on two chairs. In the summer time we had a large round tin bin filled with sawdust and raised from the ground by two bricks. I got the bag of sawdust from the local funeral parlour, which I mostly carried over my shoulder; thankfully it was only a few houses down from the lane.

You put the handle of the sweeping brush into the centre of the bin and gradually filled the bin tightly with dampened sawdust and removed the brush handle carefully, then newspaper was pushed underneath the bin and lit slowly. The smoke ascended and the centre reddened and a little flame appeared at the top of the bin, and this smouldered for hours.

You then placed two flat iron bars across the bin and put your large pot on top to boil, some cold water in your bath and a bar of soap and started washing. Whites and cleanest clothes went in first, and the whites were often boiled on top of the bin, allowing you extra hot water. Sometimes a blue bag was used to whiten clothes. Everything was rinsed finally in cold water, and weather favourable, all were line dried, otherwise on backs of chairs around the fire or from a string line across the kitchen.

Baby nappies were always a problem you used so many mine were often made from old sheets cut in squares and hemmed.

I loved to watch my completed wash blowing on the line and gathering them in my arms and smelling the freshness. Sitting by the turf fire at night I folded them in my lap and aired them.

I adjusted very well to married life, in spite of everything. I liked responsibility, and enjoyed a challenge. I was strong willed, yet sensitive (a difficult combination).

Andy was the complete opposite to me in character. After his weekly contribution of £2 was handed over to me, there his responsibility ended.

He had no interest at all in family life; his friends, the pub and dance halls were more important to him. In his mind he was still a single man and, the baby and I were just in the background.

He was not an affectionate man. I had this tremendous amount of love to give and it was so frustrating, this was my first boy friend and I loved him. This was the man that in my naivety was going to die for me, who switched overnight to a stranger. I just could not confide in anyone, I would be told, "You made your bed."

I was starved of love and he was uncomfortable if I displayed any affection, I actually thought that perhaps this was common and mostly everybody's lot, not realising at the time that this was a very important part of marriage. So I was now beginning to accept this situation, probably out of shyness and embarrassment. When Noel was 11 months I became pregnant with my second baby.

By this time I was visiting mammy and grandmother's house regularly taking Noel in the pram, while doing my shopping. So they all had a good insight into my situation. Grandmother would remark to my auntie how thin or tired I looked. They did that in those days, and often talked about you as if you weren't there, but were always concerned for me.

I was now 19 and realising how much I was missing out on, seeing all my school and work pals still carefree and going to dances, and doing all the things I should still be doing. Still I had my lovely baby Noel and that compensated for a lot. I was able to give all my love to him. He was a beautiful child and starting to stand up and crawl.

I met most other young couples on Sundays, often together out walking with their babies, but Andy never accompanied me.

REMEMBERING MY GRANDMOTHER'S BOARDING HOUSE

Being a very exciting place, meeting so many different people, life was never dull. Lodgers came from different walks of life - railway men, electricians, builders.

As a young girl aged 13 and enjoyed running all the errands, especially on Friday nights, when they were all paid. I was in great demand and it meant pocket money.

It was usually razor blades, coal tar soap, olive oil, Brylcreem, cigarettes and matches I was sent to purchase, and as a rule I could keep the change. This gave me the money for the pictures or often school books.

I spent a lot of time in my grandmother's house. She was an aristocratic-looking lady: lovely face, grey hair, worn brushed back in a neat bun at the nape of her neck. Being the first grandchild we had a special relationship and I always slept with her.

I would answer the rosary which she recited on black beads as each bead slipped through her fingers repeating the five decades. Coming near Christmas it would be a special prayer (the Hail and Blessed) to be said for thirty days before Christmas for a special intention. She yawned a lot while praying as if she was very weary as indeed I expect she was.

❇

It was hard work preparing vegetables, baking, getting lunches ready, setting and clearing tables. We had coal fires then, and were busy cleaning out grates, breaking sticks, making beds. I recall carrying with my auntie a large wicker basket six flights upstairs to change all the beds. There was a bucket

for slops and it was basin and jugs then placed on washstands
- no bathrooms.

It was outside toilets and chamber pots in bedrooms in
those days. Beds were stripped, every week the linen basket
filled, mattress turned and eiderdown shaken. The basket of
clean linen for each bed was refilled - 14 of them. All the
eiderdowns were then folded back neatly on the end of each
bed. Then the laundry book was taken out to count sheets,
pillow slips and bedspreads before they were sent off for the
next week's wash.

My aunt had small children whom I helped to take care
of. What a busy house that was, with lots of laughter and
witty jokes. The bakery man arrived daily with fresh bread,
shouting in the hall, "How many today Ma'am?"

Milk was delivered by horse and cart. You purchased six
pennyworth or maybe a shilling's worth and it was transferred from a large container with a ladle. The apple man also
delivered eating and cooking apples from his horse drawn
cart, and sometimes eggs and vegetables.

Bags of coal were delivered by the coalman covered in
coal dust, going straight through the front hall into the back
hall where the heavy bag was eased from his shoulders and
emptied into the large dark coal house. He was often singing
and whistling away and good humouredly giving my uncle a
tip for a horse on the race of the day.

My uncle was physically handicapped. He never went
to school. Grandmother was so protective of him. He taught

himself to read from the bill posts across the road from the house.

He loved books and talking to the lodgers about world events. In later years he was on local radio in Dublin and often referred to as a 'walking encyclopaedia'. I loved him so much, he was so witty.

There was a big carnival held in the people's park in late August and September - great entertainment, with a trapeze, dancing, magicians, fortune tellers. It always attracted large crowds, lots of music, it was very exciting.

An Italian man comes easily to mind, he stayed at my grandmother's for the full 3 weeks of the carnival, accompanied by a beautiful Italian lady, I suspected she was his girl friend. I was then aged 14, and I got a crush on him at first sight. It was so painful to go through, and it was my secret.

The house having no bathroom, he often brushed his teeth in the yard near the water tap, and spat into the drain after continually washing out his mouth. One morning I stood at the back door just gazing at him. He was so handsome - black hair and wonderful teeth that sparkled when he smiled.

On that particular day, turning around, he managed to pass me. I was rooted to the ground. He winked at me and in broken English said, "I would like to come back and see you when you're 18." My heart missed a beat, I felt weak at the knees. Knowing that he had noticed me was enough to keep me going for the day. I flew through the work in the house.

I kept a scrapbook, in which I collected pictures of my favourite film stars - Robert Taylor, Barbara Stanwyck, Olivia de Havilland, Vivien Leigh, Clark Gable, Humphrey Bogart, Edward G. Robinson and James Cagney. Grandmother called it "a book of bad girls".

I liked entertaining my little cousins, especially on a wet Sunday afternoon when it was usually quiet. Grandmother would be having her nap and Auntie would be in her bedroom sitting in the window, knitting for the boys.

❋

The living room window conveniently had a very deep window seat about two feet deep, it made a good stage for me to perform for my cousins. I put a lot of chairs around the window making sure they could see me.

Heavy velvet curtains draped the window and hung from a wooden pole with brass rings so that they could be drawn and pulled back easily. Screwing a cup hook in to the side of the window, I got a heavy top coat from the hall stand and hung it from the hook, then slipped on one of auntie's long nightdresses.

Shaking my long dark hair loose to fall over one side of my face, Barbara Stanwyck style, I was almost ready for the show. Closing the curtains after instructing my little cousins to keep watching the screen, I swished back the curtains announcing the film, *His Affair*. The coat was Robert Taylor, and I was Barbara.

Throwing the sleeves of the coat over my shoulders, I was being embraced by 'Robert'. He was in prison and I was visiting him (bearing in mind I had a vivid imagination), acting out the scene as in the film, crying and calling him "a dirty low down contemptible stool pigeon," and shouting as if shaking the prison bars, "Guard, guard let me out of here," allowing my mouth to droop at the sides, as Barbara's did in the film. My cousins' eyes were riveted on me.

I then stepped down on the floor, singing softly as I glided between the chairs (I hum a waltz "bo, bo, bo, bo, bo, bo, bo, bo, the music plays, you're in my arms, and as we dance...." At this point the door suddenly opened. It was my uncle asking what the hell was going on with grandmother trying to rest. So that finished the show. But not before my little cousins were put under pressure to clap for me.

I was in my own little world of make-believe, if only for an hour. My cousins were entertained, though not really understanding what was going on. I'm sure they would have preferred a show of cowboys and Indians. One of my cousins now living in Toronto still recalls the performance fondly, and laughs very heartily about it.

※

The time always came of course when I had to return to my own home, still being school age, mammy and daddy complained if I stayed too long at my grandmother's as there were still chores to be done at home, like rounding up the younger ones in the evening. They were like steps of stairs, so close in age. I would prepare their feeds and get them to bed.

I didn't appreciate having to go to bed with the two youngest with a bottle of cocoa in one hand and a dummy in the other. I would make sure I had a magazine called *The Oracle* or *Miracle,* popular at that period of time for teenagers. I had to hide it. Daddy did not approve of these books filling my head with rubbish, but they were just simple little love stories.

One baby lay close to my back sucking her dummy, and I prayed they would soon drop off to sleep, giving me some peace to concentrate on my love stories and dream myself to sleep, perhaps thinking maybe some day when I grew up things like that would happen to me, and I would be happy ever after.

I was never really bored. Aged 14, the painful years when I was beginning to be noticed by boys, and I in turn looked at them - the inbetween years - so confusing.

I had to wait at table when the lodgers came for meals. I would often hear the odd remark as to how quickly I was growing into a pretty young woman. I would blush, being very shy still. On my way back to the kitchen passing the hall stand that had a centre mirror, I would toss my hair and glance at my face.

Waiting for the tray of dessert to carry back into the dining room on one occasion, grandmother noticed me tightening my belt around my waist, struggling to reach the next hole on the buckle.

She was quite horrified, remarking to my aunt, "Good Lord, what is the world coming to at all? I just caught Brigid arranging her belt, going in to the men." The year was 1939.

My aunt had four boys and two girls not more than 12 or 14 months between them. The three youngest were boys who had to be assisted to the toilet. They referred to their penis as their 'man'. Inevitably I would be called to take them to the toilet and take out their 'man'. They wore short knitted trousers. Now I was starting to grow up and didn't like the idea. I said to my aunt, "I really don't want to do that any more."

Both grandmother and auntie were highly amused and went into peals of laughter. I recall being very embarrassed about the whole business. In later years that story was related to the boys by my aunt when I was visiting them. The one with a good sense of humour looked at me and said, "Brigid, you certainly wouldn't take it out now?" Well there really wasn't any answer to that. We laughed for a long time about the stories of the old times.

At the end of a busy day, with all the work done and breakfast table set, grandmother would retire upstairs, where she had a great view from the window of people passing.

There was a cinema almost in view and lots of people passed by on their way to the pictures, especially if there was a good film on.

Auntie would be busy bathing the children in the big tin bath before bed. I would comb grandmother's long hair and often plait it. She loved that and found it very relaxing. Or maybe I would hold a long coil of wool stretched across both hands as she wound it into a loose ball for knitting or crocheting.

I cannot remember ever being idle and having nothing to do. Always when I got back to my own home at night there were always jobs waiting to be done.

※

I had my school bag to keep in order, homework to do, and lots of shoes to polish for school.

The weekends I nearly always spent at grandmother's and I would have six flights of stairs to dust down. It had thick green lino (called inlaid) it was held securely in place with flat brass rods secured by a fitting at each end. They had to be polished with Brasso.

I was a bit of an exhibitionist. I sang *Sweet Sixteen*, or some other popular song of the day, hoping the kitchen door was open and I was impressing and entertaining them all as they worked preparing tea for the lodgers. And I was always out of tune.

Anyway on one such day my ego took a tumble when my uncle shouted up the stairs, "Brigid, are you in pain? I can give you an aspirin." I replied, "No, I'm okay Jim, only singing," deciding he must be stupid.

Then there was the long tiled hall to be scrubbed and mats to be beaten against the wall in the yard that you approached through the back hall that led to the coal house. I always started at the front door step with a large basin of hot water that was achieved by boiling a kettle. No running hot water in those days.

Armed with a floor cloth, Vim powder and scrubbing brush, not forgetting something to kneel on, and my little rubber apron, I was all set to go.

The psychology in that house was something to be reckoned with. Grandmother and auntie would stand at the end of the stairway supposed to be in conversation about something or other, but making sure I was in earshot. Then the remarks would be something like this, "My God, isn't she a good child, a great little worker, now watch her rinse the cloth and give it a second wash, I bet she will change the water before finishing the hall."

※

Water was dutifully changed and the conversation continued. "God bless her, what would we do without Brigid?' Hall completed I went back out to the step, throwing the very dirty water down the pathway. With yard brush in hand I continued to ease the water onto the road. Door brasses and window sills were left to the next day.

The house had a big red tiled kitchen: large scrubbed dresser with cupboard and a big matching table, large wooden arm chair placed near the fire, a huge range with chrome fender and matching stools, and brasslike pennies surrounding the fire place. Over that were pewter dish covers hanging here and there. The room also had a big electric cooker. Just before the entrance to the pantry where there was a shallow stone sink, wooden table, a long string across the ceiling used to air clothes on, an old fashioned washing machine and wringer, and at the end of the long pantry, an old stove.

There was no garden just a yard with pulley lines, the outside toilet, a tap for water and underneath a large wooden barrel, full of water.

During one of the winter nights my grandmother gave me a hot water bottle to put in our bed - it was a very cold house. I was first in bed, enjoying the comfort of the bottle all to myself, lying on my back, hot water bottle on my tummy with both arms wrapped around it. Suddenly the stopper popped out and the hot water ran down my tummy. I soon jumped out of bed and opening the door I ran down 5 flights of stairs none too quietly shouting, "I'm burned, I'm burned!" Some of the lodgers opened their bedroom doors to see what the commotion was all about. They just got a glimpse of my nightie flying by.

Reaching the end of the stairs I flew straight into my grandmother's arms. She asked, "Brigid, in the name of God, what is the matter with you? You have the house in an uproar!" I was sobbing, "I'm burned!" Grandmother not understanding how it happened, and I trying to explain through the sobs.

❋

My auntie busied herself mixing bicarbonate of soda with water in a bowl. I was taken back upstairs to bed again, lying on my back and this mixture of bicarb was swiftly applied to my tummy by my aunt.

I was being scolded in no uncertain terms as to the silly girl I was to squeeze a hot water bottle. They were afraid of pneumonia from shock and worried as to what my parents would think about this. My grandmother was feeling my forehead and trying to console me and keep me warm. However, I was none the worse from this experience, but wasn't trusted again with a hot water bottle. I remembered that incident for a long time to come.

My beloved grandmother died in her sleep in November, 1947 aged 74 years. I was by this time married with three children myself.

I will always cherish the memories of my grandmother's boarding house.

ALL THAT SEEMS SO LONG AGO

However, I was learning to knit now too, and making little matinee coats. Andy's sister was a good knitter so I picked up a lot from her. We knit without a pattern, which was quite clever: V necks, raglan sleeves and turning the heel of a sock.

His mother was mainly the cook and she would shop for the meat daily in Murphys Butchers on the hill. It would be 1 shilling 3p worth of steak each for Andy and Madge's husband, and 1 shilling 6p worth of stewing beef for us. We pooled the money every day.

She produced nice tarts from the little oven, also bread pudding, which was boiled in a large cotton cloth tied with string and boiled for hours. It had to be watched and kept boiling to insure water didn't get into the pudding. When ready, the cloth was removed and this large pudding transferred to a plate. It tasted and looked very good. In nice weather this was boiled on the sawdust bin.

At this stage I was looking for someplace new to live, with a second baby on the way, we needed more space. I succeeded in getting a fairly big room with a Mrs. Walsh, in a nice area of town, but again on the top of a four storey house with no cooker just a small grate to cook on, but she was a nice kind lady.

The sticks to light the fire had to be broken in the yard and I carried the baby under one arm and the bucket with sticks in the other hand. Mrs. Walsh usually looked after Noel while I broke sticks in the back yard and often those times Andy would be washing and shaving upstairs preparing to go out and the baby would be in his way.

Mrs. Walsh was so disgusted with him and she made no attempt to hide it either and would remark as he passed down the stairs, "It's a shame to see that pregnant young girl breaking sticks and carrying a baby up and down stairs," but he wasn't a sensitive man.

I went into labour on my second baby, August 8th at 11:30 p.m. Andy had not long come in, so I packed my little bag, Mrs. Walsh looked after Noel, who was asleep. I hated leaving him but Andy's mother was going to take care of him until I came home.

Andy suggested I got up on the bar of the bike, he tied my bag on the back and he cycled to the hospital. We had to pass the ballroom, and the dancers were beginning to come out. Nearing midnight I asked him to let me off the bike as I had a pain, and he replied, "Not here with everyone coming out of the dance. You will be alright until you get to the hospital."

I let the pain wash over me, and I was alright. When we arrived, Andy knocked on the hospital door, cycling off before the nurse even opened the door. I was 24 hours in labour, but had a normal birth at 11 p.m. August 9th 1945. Returning home again after 10 days I had Noel back. We called the second baby Joseph, after my father. He was a difficult baby to bring up, continually crying at night

Joseph was a month old when there was a carnival in the city park on 8th September 1945. It was on a Sunday and not far from where I lived. After dinner Andy had gone out as usual and I decided to take the babies to the park. I settled Joseph down in the pram and dressed Noel up in his blue and white suit and little white boots. He looked lovely that day, he had blonde hair that hung loose below his ears and a sausage curl on top. He was standing on a chair as I dressed him and I held him out from me and told him how beautiful he was. I then sat him at the end of the pram and off we went to the park.

During the carnival Noel didn't look well and he vomited. I rushed home with him at about 4 o'clock and Mrs. Walsh advised me to get a doctor. She looked after both babies while I ran for the doctor.

I just got him, as he was leaving for the races, and he wasn't happy about being called out. But he gave Noel a quick examination and prescribed a worm powder for him.

It was common then for a doctor to tell you your child had a worm fever. Then getting his medical bag together in a hurry for the races, he asked me if it was convenient for me to pay him. I was so mad at his attitude. I said, "No it was not convenient for me to pay now." It was 10 shillings and I didn't have it anyway.

I made Noel as comfortable as I could in bed, he was very hot and I knew he had a high temperature. My mind was racing now as to where I could locate his father, leaving the babies again to get the prescription – I didn't know where to go on a Sunday. Mrs Walsh took over while I made my way to Andy's mother's house, hoping she might know where Andy was.

She came back to the room with me and eventually Andy came in, not pleased the child was sick, and everything was my fault. By Monday Noel had deteriorated Andy went to work as usual. I called another doctor and he diagnosed pneumonia. On Tuesday morning he called again and Noel had developed meningitis, I remember screaming and beating my hands against the wall, "No, no, no, doctor this can't be."

The doctor was taken back at my reaction, and said, "This sometimes happens in a crisis, so he could pull through." Noel died at 3 o'clock on Thursday 12th September 1945 aged 18 months. I couldn't believe it, my beautiful baby dead. My sister Margaret had died aged 14 in May that year, again meningitis, so it was all too familiar to me.

I was in the room with Noel when he died. Mrs. Coleman across the road from the house was also there; Mrs. Walsh had called her and she held my hand. Standing by the cot I actually saw his lovely little face light up and Mrs. Coleman closed both his eyes and said, "Pray for your mammy now, love."

I was in shock it was all over in 4 days. I lost my baby. My grandmother and my father were in the room soon after, I can't remember anything else. Someone did call Andy from work and I was aware he was there and his mother and sister. Daddy put his hands on my shoulder as I sat by Noel's cot feeling numb. I said, "I can't live without Noel," and daddy said, "You can girl, you have to."

I had to live without Margaret, she wanted someone to mind in heaven so she took Noel. I sat with him all night someone put a veil over the cot. It was September time and there were flies about. I was feeling his hair through the bars of the cot. Some people stayed, I don't remember who. I didn't go to the funeral, I couldn't bear to see him go down in the ground. It was 1 o'clock Friday when I leaned out of the window to see the little white coffin being carried in to the car by Andy. Joseph was in the pram, and I thought, "I can't look after you, please God help me, I feel so empty, so alone." Everything was unreal. I ached inside.

AFTER MY BABY'S DEATH

The days dragged on and I looked in a different way at Joseph. He was a helpless little baby and I loved him, but I felt so drained, physically and emotionally. I had no energy or enthusiasm and Andy didn't seem capable of even sharing the grief. I can't remember him consoling me, not even remotely and he coped with it as before, by going out nightly.

Of course I couldn't stay in the same house; everything I looked at or touched reminded me of Noel. The doctor was kind and later called to see me and said, "Your baby will be an ambassador for you in heaven." Lovely thought but it did nothing to console me at the time.

We then moved to an even smaller room up town on an estate. I didn't care much at the time where I was, Joseph had every illness you could think of and I was so busy and concerned for him that it eased the longing for Noel. Joseph was constantly crying, night and day, and this wasn't making life any easier with Andy. I was expected to know why Joseph was crying, especially at night. Patience wasn't one of his virtues.

Then at 4 months old Joseph had a convulsion; he stiffened in the cot and was frothing from the mouth. I got the doctor straight away, my sister in law lived down the road, I called her and both of us were waiting when the doctor arrived. He asked me to wait outside as I was very upset and he confirmed convulsions.

He gave Joseph an injection and his arm swelled slightly, the doctor was pleased about that it meant he was reacting positively. But he stressed that Joseph was very sick and told me to phone him in the morning if he was still with us. The doctor was surprised to get a call next morning to say Joseph was still alive. He was very pleased and called again straight away and kept a close watch on the baby as he slowly recovered, with careful nursing. This child was now filling my life easing still more the loss of Noel.

Nothing was getting better in the marriage and it was so easy to start a big row about something silly. I left Andy when Joseph was 8 months old, I just couldn't cope with him; he was so domineering and demanding. I was still shattered after the loss of my lovely baby, and looking after a sick child. So I went home to my mother with Joseph though I didn't want to, with daddy unemployed and a lot of children in the house I wasn't welcomed with open arms.

But I couldn't think of anything else to do, and they understood. I had to sleep on the kitchen table with the baby. Mammy spread an old blanket over it with 2 pillows, and an old eiderdown to cover us that she borrowed from my grandmother. It was a wide table, just as well.

Again Joseph wasn't well, one of his eyes became very inflamed and I was bathing it in borasic powder. Then he got bronchitis, and up and down to the doctor, but I nursed him through it.

Making myself useful in the house baking soda bread and helping mammy generally, I was doing all I could, trying to make up for the inconvenience of being there.

Andy was back with his mother and refusing to support us. He called at our house one evening, mammy and daddy were out and I was on my own with Joseph. Andy was abusive saying, "You walked out, so you can walk back."

We had a string line across the kitchen to air clothes on, and the skirt of my wedding suit was thrown over it, I wore it a lot as I didn't have a lot of clothes. In a rage he pulled it off the line and put it under his shoe, ripping it, saying, "You won't be going anywhere in that." Then he left.

From then on my sister called down to his house every Friday night and he did give her £2 a week for a few weeks. Then he sent notes saying he was sorry and that he had applied to the corporation for a house, as we were separated and had no place to live.

In the meantime his sister had got a house in Collins Avenue and Andy was in the house on his own with his mother. I couldn't continue sleeping on a table at home and things were getting uncomfortable so I went back to his mother's home. There was more room in the house now and his mother was soon to move in with her daughter. She was getting a job and her mother was to take care of her children. Andy was reasonable for awhile but still went out every night, and soon fell in to his old habits.

My third baby Mags, was born October 1946, a breach birth, and a tiny baby, just 5.5 lbs. She also had a convulsion at 3 months but not as severe as Joseph's. She couldn't keep cod liver oil down, so I massaged it in to her body in front of the fire at night. I was convinced she would absorb it and maybe she did, as she slowly improved.

I plodded on, calling Andy early, putting his bike outside the door, and generally being a good wife, and his mother called in often. Mary was born 25th September 1948 weighing 8lbs, a healthy baby I didn't have much trouble rearing Mary.

We were still waiting on news of our council house. I needed more space badly now with three children and looking forward to having an electric cooker. Coal was scarce I collected slack from the coal depot and rolled it up on the bike, it was all uphill. Dampened down, it kept the fire going for a long time.

We had concrete floors and you could buy 2p worth of red raddle from hardware store close by, mix it in a bucket of cold water and apply it to the floor. It was hard work and your arms were red to your elbows, but once completed and a nice turf fire going, it made everything cosy and welcoming.

I then found out I was expecting my fourth child. Billy was born April 1950, a very small baby 5.5lbs and hard to rear. He didn't keep his food down, wasn't gaining weight, and was hospitalised for observation for a few weeks. A heart murmur was suspected, eventually he was cleared of that, and came home and was slow to gain weight but apart from the usual childhood ailments he thrived. Still plodding along with the sawdust bin collecting the slack balanced on the push bike together with the turf made us a nice warm fire.

During this period of time Andy was on strike. He was prominent and active in the unions and strikes were very common. The parish Priest would try to intervene in the disputes that arose between workers and management.

On one such occasion in a discussion with Andy the Priest described him as "an aggravator and a dictator". Personally I would think that summed him up pretty well.

❋

He was now putting his time into fishing and hunting in the country with his mates, and would ask for his dinner to be ready at a certain time. That day the fire went against me and I took a long time to get it started.

His dinner was for 1 o'clock, chips and sausages. I was struggling with this pan of chips while coaxing the fire to flame, when I heard his steps coming down the path, knowing there was going to be a big row when he saw his dinner wasn't on the table.

True to form he took the pan of half cooked chips and slung them all over the floor. The children were crying and looking at the mess. He went back out, banging the door behind him, and I could hear his voice passing all the little houses, doors were usually left open then. He was chatting to neighbours remarking on the nice weather, very good for fishing – a very different person to the man that just left his home.

Joseph ran out after him, shouting, "Daddy you're a pig you just spilt my dinner." As I cleaned up that mess all I could think of saying was, 'Dear Jesus, if nobody else knows, you know mental cruelty is so hard to prove.'

On another occasion while pregnant with Billy I was standing over a bath of washing supported on two chairs while he was polishing his shoes, complaining about something before going out for the evening. Suddenly he threw the polish cloth in my face. With the steam of the water it clung to my face and by the time I had got the cloth off he had gone out the door. I remember just looking at the closed door and thinking, 'If a car runs you down on the road I'll be glad,' and I meant it.

I got our parish Priest one day to call on him but Andy just pushed the Priest out of the way and walked out.

No social services those days, there was simply no escape.

❊

My sister Lena went to England when she was 15. Mammy arranged a job for her through the nuns, in a convent in Middlesex, and she was sending money home. Lena was 19 when she wrote, saying she had met this nice Englishman, and asking if she could bring him home on holiday as he longed to see Ireland.

Mammy was rushing around, freshening up the house and preparing the parlour for him, which had a single bed and wardrobe and was used as a bedroom. They were on good terms with our next door neighbour, Mrs Dowling, so mammy called to her over the back garden hedge, where they often had a chat, asking if she could borrow a china cup and saucer for our visitor from England.

Our cups were common white and still mostly without handles. Mrs Dowling obliged and gave mammy the cup and saucer on a tray.

So they were all warned not to let our visitor go upstairs, not to call down for the coats for the bed if he was around and especially not to call for the bucket, which was usually left on the landing for their convenience.

Anyway Len arrived; this Englishman was causing quite a stir in the house they were all warned to be on their best behaviour. The morning after his arrival mammy went to get the tray and china to give Len his breakfast and couldn't find the cup and saucer.

I had one sister, Nieve, who was a bit of a featherhead, and not very tactful to say the least, and mammy told her to look for the cup with the handle.

My sister knocked at the parlour door and Len said, "Good morning duck," and my sister replied, "Good morning Len. Is there a cup with a handle in there?" He said, "Pardon duck?" My mother was speechless, trying to get her hands on Nieve but she was too quick and escaped out the front door, realising the blunder she had made. Anyway, the cup with the handle was found and all was well.

❈

We often talked about our sister Margaret who used to take an old pram we had and collect sticks in the country for firewood. One day on returning home with her pile of sticks, daddy was getting her meal ready, which was a boiled egg, bread and margarine, and Margaret said, "I can't eat that egg, daddy I don't like it, I'd prefer a cake."

As there was no money to buy her a cake, daddy had a brainwave. He cooled the egg under the tap and sent it back to Condon's shop across the road, where we were very well known as we used this shop regularly. After a bit of persuasion, Agnes Condon, who was very good hearted but very abrupt said, "Your father is a bloody nuisance," but she gave him the cake and took the egg back.

It was only about a week after that when one of our neighbours was coming out of Condon's shop and was chatting away to my sister confiding in her they would not be buying eggs in Condon's again because they were cooked when you got them! Daddy thought that was very funny, when relating it to Mammy, imagine O'Brien's ended up with the cooked egg. "It would have been nice to be a fly on the wall when he returned the egg to Agnes."

THERE WAS A GOOD PICTURE ON CALLED WATERLOO BRIDGE

Robert Taylor and Vivian Leigh were the stars and I was excited about seeing it as I so seldom went out in the evening. I arranged with my friend Elsie that we go together, told Andy I was going to the pictures and he objected of course and told me my place was at home with my children.

But I was determined I was going and arranged with my sister to baby sit and the neighbour next door to keep an eye on them as well. Off I went.

I had got the children to bed first, the eldest Joseph was 5 then. I got home after having enjoyed the film, but Andy came home unusually early, sent my sister home, and waited for me.

When I got there he physically and verbally abused me, and threw me out the front door. This would be about 11:30 at night.

Joseph jumped out of bed and ran out after me. I picked him up in my arms, as he had no shoes on, to make my way across the road to Andy's brother's and borrowed a coat and shoes for Joseph, explaining what had happened. They asked me to go back and said they would come with me, and I agreed as Mags, Mary and Billy were in bed.

Andy's brother and wife opened the door and we went in, but he caught me and threw me out again, I attempted to walk home but mammy's house was all up hill, it was now midnight, so I decided to walk to my grandmother's instead, where we both spent the night. I returned home the next morning when I knew Andy would be gone to work, leaving the children in the charge of my neighbour.

There was another scene that evening when he came home from work, throwing his weight around, telling me I could go anytime I liked. He was dead safe telling me that, knowing full well I would never leave the children. He had the ability to create a scene causing an atmosphere, making it impossible for us to hold a conversation. He then came and went as he liked, he was very tactical.

I never knew whether to be up or in bed when he came in. There was a row if I was in bed. The shoes were taken off and slung across the kitchen so it was pot luck. If he had some of his friends with him and a few bottles of Guinness consumed, he was usually pleasant.

If he did look after the children on Sunday morning while I went to mass he would tell me not to hang around talking with my friends, as he was waiting to go out.

Conversation was always a strain; you got absolutely nowhere if it was about clothes for the children, I was told we looked okay to him. Nothing was ever discussed or worked out; all those things were my problem.

❈

We were awaiting our allotment of a corporation house and looking forward to a new area and more conveniences as we had no garden or electric cooker in this house it was very basic.

I wasn't feeling good myself, complaining of indigestion pains, and my side ached. I was under 8 stone.

I got the pain bad one afternoon and was vomiting. As I had no money to pay a doctor to call to the house, Andy's brother and his wife offered to call the doctor. It was 10 shillings. He diagnosed gallstones and then there was a prescription to get. I had to pledge my wedding ring to pay for that, 30 shillings, and it was never redeemed. I was on a special diet and it was possible I may eventually have to have an operation.

Conditions were unsettled in the factory where Andy worked and he would often casually remark, "If this continues I'm off to England."

Joseph had at this stage started school, but he hated going to school in the morning. I recall one morning walking him to school, giving him a hug, reassuring him he was going to have a lovely day. I hated to see him unhappy. Your first child starting school is always hard to let go.

Andy's mates all seemed to have good marriages all had their priorities right where their families were concerned but it never seemed to rub off on him.

We were eventually allotted a corporation house, a 3 bedroom bungalow and I was relieved. We had a pantry with a sink and cooker, a nice range in the living room and the house was on a nice wide street and the neighbours were friendly. The children were delighted, lots of friends to play with, so my heart was lighter.

Andy still very much taken up with the unions at work and sometimes away weekends at meetings but for a while took an interest in the back garden and some evenings did a bit of digging in the garden before going out later.

❋

He kept a small old leather case under the bed that was locked and he always returned the key to his pocket, his excuse was he had things in there he didn't want to lose and the children might get to them.

Nevertheless it did interest me. I guessed he had money in it. One evening he was doing some work in the garden and his coat was hanging on the door, key in the pocket.

Having no money and a lot needed in the house after moving, I kept him in view through the window, opened the case, heart racing, and sure enough there before my eyes was £35 - a fortune in 1952. I took £5 which was twice my house-keeping money, locked the case put the key back, got the children ready and went off shopping. I bought things that were all novelties to us, like smoked rashers, eggs, sausages and wool to knit.

As I pushed the pram up the hill fully loaded, coming towards me on the same path was Andy. The first thought I had was, 'He has missed the money and came looking for me,' but he strolled past us, saying he would be home for tea at six O' clock. So I relaxed. Now it was Saturday afternoon, and knowing I was safe for another while we all enjoyed the nice fresh bread rashers and eggs.

About a week later my sister called to look after the children as I needed to go to confession. There was a mission on, so I went to one of the missioners and confessed I stole the money from my husband's case.

He said, "My child did he have much money?" I replied, "Yes, Father." "Why then didn't you take it all? That's your money so if you get a chance, take more." I replied, "No Father, he would kill me." I think he was amused. Anyway he gave me absolution and asked me to pray for him. I in turn said, "You had better pray for me." But I felt safe now, knowing I hadn't committed a mortal sin. Andy never did miss that money but I never chanced it again, I wasn't going to push my luck.

❋

The children were settling well at school and making friends in the street. Billy was popular with the neighbours as he was quiet and well mannered. Joseph was mostly with his cousin Tommy.

Mags had the girls next door and Mary joined them. Joseph continued to have different ailments, complaining a lot of earaches and headaches. I worried about him a lot since the convulsions; losing my baby was never far from my mind, so I was inclined to overreact when the children got sick.

Now aged 27 and still getting indigestion pains I was diagnosed as having gallstones and operated on in our local hospital, which was about 3 miles walk all up hill from our home. I left home that morning at 8:45 carrying my brown paper parcel containing the essentials; my nightdress, towel, soap etc. Admission time was 10:00 a.m. and my mother-in-law was taking care of the children for me.

Mary was very attached to me, and her little face was pressed against the window, waving to me and the tears streaming down her face. I hated leaving the 4 of them. Arriving at the hospital I was glad to sit down on the chair placed outside the ward, waiting to be admitted. A staff nurse soon appeared, looking very efficient; the hospitals in those days were run by nuns and had very strict rules.

I was detained for 7 days before the operation as I was underweight. I was given milk and Guinness and lots of milky foods to nourish me. One nurse especially was very kind and became a great friend.

The morning of the operation I was the first patient into theatre, which was on a level with the ward. I was 3 hours in theatre. As I was being wheeled in the nurse asking the other patients to say the rosary for me. The doctor came later in the day to tell me I had an inflamed appendix and 100 gallstones which he held up for me to see in a jam jar.

❄

I remember being so weak I had no voice, again my nurse comes to mind as she was spoon feeding me with tripe and onions, and often missed her lunch break to stay with me - a truly dedicated nurse. The rosary was recited every night by one of the nurses on duty.

I knew I was getting stronger when I could eventually answer the Hail Mary. My special nurse later became a nun and has since gone to her heavenly reward.

I was worried about the children though I knew they were in good hands. Billy was the baby then, 2 years old and easy to look after. Mary was 4 and so upset when I was leaving. Mags and Joseph were school age so they would get by. My own mother had a 4 year old and 3 children still at school and was working a few hours a day in a hotel in the city.

I was 3 weeks in hospital and wasn't fit for much when I got home. It was a struggle to get up in the morning and getting Joseph and Mags ready for school was a big ordeal. I had to sit to comb Mag's hair. Andy was mad one morning as they were both running late for school and feeling so low I couldn't even answer him back, but he had no compassion whatsoever.

I couldn't stand to make the bread, and was sitting mixing my dough in a small enamel basin when the doctor called. I could only cry when I saw him, and remember saying, "I'm so weak doctor," and he agreed I would be as I had had major surgery and it would take some time still to recover.

Andy's dinner had to be on the table when he came in from work at 1p.m. and cool enough for him to eat, otherwise he would take the plate, open the window and balance it on the windowsill, my heart in my mouth in case it fell out the window into the yard. Then it turned into a nasty row with no consideration for the children, and less for me.

❋

Nanny would bring the shopping for me as she collected her own; although she knew he was a tyrant she would be very anxious for me to please and humour him.

Andy's holidays soon came around from work and he announced he was going on holiday to England with his friend Mick Dalton for two weeks, no thought at all about leaving us. This book could not give enough scope to explain how tactical he was, no let up, so by being continuously unpleasant, he was always more or less free to come and go as he liked, with no explaining to do.

OUR NEW HOUSE

In 1952 there were new houses being built in the city centre, 3 bedrooms and a bathroom rent 21 shillings weekly. The bungalow I was in was damp and Joseph suffered with bronchitis, so I had a doctor's letter recommending me for one of these houses. My mother's uncle was in the corporation and with influence eventually I was allotted one of these houses. I was delighted. This gave me such a lift. Just imagine a bathroom! I think I always had it at the back of my mind that this new house would change Andy, but how naive of me. We moved in and soon I was to become pregnant with my 6th child.

In April, 1954 Andy left for England. The industrial strikes still continued in the factory with redundancies to follow. It was the year I was pregnant that Andy decided to go to England with 3 of his pals from the city, early 1954 he was packing to go and the children were upset of course, their daddy was going away.

At that age their daddy was important to them; Joseph was 9, Mags 7, Mary 6, Billy 4, and a new baby expected in June.

Andy had a £25 leaving fund, a lot of money in 1954. But he didn't ask me if I had a 1p for the gas or see that I was left secure in any way financially, only saying he would write as soon as he found employment, and send some money.

Lena my sister, now married and living in England, was in touch with me. She had a young son and offered to come home and look after the children while I was in hospital, and she did come.

Annie was born the 4th of June, 1954 and again a difficult birth. It was a Monday morning and there were complications with the afterbirth.

My doctor was at 9 o'clock mass and was called out. I remember the mask being put over my face from behind and when I woke up again I had a lovely baby girl, weighing over 10lbs. She was getting lots of attention because the eyes were open and she had lots of blonde hair. You were detained for

10 days after a confinement in those days and the baby was usually christened from hospital.

Andy was informed of the birth and we agreed on a name. She was a healthy baby, and pretty, as indeed all my children were. I was 29 then. My sister stayed with me for a week after I came out of hospital. I collected orange juice and cod liver oil from the clinic; they were free as the health care had improved to a great extent.

Billy was now 4 and had started school my mind was on him a lot as he was a timid, nervous child. Lena sent me her pram and some clothes for the baby by rail, all in good condition, and I was knitting more clothes when I could afford the wool. During the end of that summer I pushed the pram outside the front door into the garden, where Annie was greatly admired by the passers-by.

I think Billy was feeling pushed aside by all the attention this new baby was getting and he was likely to go to her pram and poke his finger in to her face or pull the dummy out of her mouth, it was a job watching him.

Billy was popular with everyone, quite unassuming he was with small build and inclined to be overlooked if Annie was around, being admired for her blonde hair and blue eyes. Billy standing by wasn't noticed these days. However we were not into child psychology then; trying to survive was enough.

Mags didn't like school and was an unpredictable child though very affectionate and hard to watch. She often mitched school, taking Billy with her, and just ramble around the town. The fact that other children were talking about their daddy didn't help at all, they missed him not being around and would often ask when he would be back. I would say," Christmas," and they would ask, "Will we get toys?" and all the usual questions children asked. They were lovely bright children.

Joseph was the wild one, very inquisitive and asked a lot of questions. He was learning to play the violin at school and loved music and Saint Theresa. He would ask me to sing and I would attempt one of Vera Lynn's numbers and he would say, "You're a lovely singer Mammy."

Mary was pretty busy watching them all and kept me informed if they were doing anything they shouldn't do. That kept her busy. Always hanging on to my skirt a clingy child, Billy was busy doing his own little thing, mostly influenced by Mags.

Andy was writing from time to time and sending £4 a week, sometimes £6 and often missed a week. I never knew if I was getting money or not. I had a book in a little corner shop which was close by, enabling me to purchase 'on tick' groceries such as flour- very important.

I baked a lot – milk, sugar, tea, eggs, and so on and vegetables and potatoes, which I mashed and cracked an egg in for nourishment. I made rice, saved stale bread for bread pudding, and jelly was a big favourite with apple tarts.

Surprisingly enough this new house I managed to furnish nicely from a big furniture store in the town for as little as 5 shillings weekly.

I had nice red lino in the hallway and stairs and broken tile effect inlaid in the living room. Three bedrooms also had lino. A nice dining room suite in the living room. Kitchen was basic with table and chairs. I was delighted to have achieved so much.

My pen and paper came out every Friday night as I balanced my money. Mostly I bought secondhand school books. The money was coming more irregularly now from England.

I was seriously considering looking for a job. But in the mid 50's it was hard for women to find work and Annie was about 11 months old. Still I felt I could make it happen if I looked hard enough. We knew of a very elderly lady in her mid 60's, a good washer woman who wore long black skirts and a black shawl and lived in a small house on her own, who was anxious to live in with a family, in preference to an old folks home.

She loved children, and when I suggested she lived with us in exchange for her bed and board looking after the children, she was delighted. I suppose you could describe her as a very wholesome old lady, Mary loved her.

Before this all happened however Mags got very sick and she was inclined to hide things from me in case I kept her in. After taking her to the doctor my worst fears were confirmed Mags was indeed sick, with a form of tuberculosis or rheumatic fever. She had little red bumps all over her body and needed complete bed rest as there was a possibility it could leave her with a heart weakness.

Mags looked pale and tired but would not give in to being sick. I had my work cut out keeping this child in bed. I brought her bed downstairs and carried her to the bathroom and back. No matter how seriously I talked to her, the little mind was working as to how she could get out of bed. It was hard to be cross as she was such a loveable child, but thank God she recovered with no ill effects to her heart and she was soon in full flight again, making the most of it.

No problems with Mary, a good child. I would describe her as having dark hair and very pretty, inclined to be shy. Joseph was busy playing marbles in the street with his friends, and Billy was mostly following Mags around, if he could catch up with her.

My friend Noeleen lived down the street from me - a pretty vivacious woman with a good sense of humour. Her husband was a fireman so she was lucky enough to have a free telephone installed. She also worked and took off on her push bike to her little part-time jobs. We were great friends, went for walks with the prams, discussed our problems and laughed a lot too. She had 6 children. Their education was very important to Noeleen and they were clever children. She felt I was too soft with mine.

I liked to decorate the house and keep it presentable so I was always busy ironing, baking, knitting. I loved the radio, especially on the dark nights when the children were bathed and in bed. Sometimes Noeleen would call for a chat.

Andy arrived home, a few days before Christmas, 1954 and the children were excited, looking forward to seeing their daddy and getting presents. Annie was 6 months then but I did send him a photo of her and I was hoping maybe after the separation he would have missed the children and maybe be more responsible. The children ran to greet him on his arrival.

What was strange really was he avoided any eye contact with me, he had presents for the children and a gift for me of a silver neck chain, still he seemed very uneasy.

He had his meal and went out later that night to meet his pals, returning late with a few of his friends and bottles of Guinness so it was a party and sing song. I eventually left them and went to bed. He was still sleeping next morning when I got up to prepare breakfast for the children, who were on holidays.

Christmas Eve morning a card arrived for Andy from England, simply signed 'Gwen.'

He explained it away by saying it was from his boss's daughter, this however didn't ring true, added to his restlessness and boasting to his friends how great England was. With no plans to take us over, or wishing he could return, I think the seed was sown then.

Andy returned to England soon after Christmas, the money was then coming very irregularly. I was friends with one of his pal's wives, she had a large family and a little shop, a kind hearted lady. I would sometimes call to ask if her money had arrived, especially if mine was late. Of course she would say, "Yes." I got mine on one occasion and I said to her, "I only get £4 a week. That's bad enough, but when it doesn't come at all is even worse." Andy and her husband both worked together in the same job and shared the same digs and she received £25 a week. She sometimes gave me some offal meat and vegetables, to make a stew for the children.

Easter soon arrived and on Easter Sunday Billy got very sick with bronchitis. I managed to get a doctor but being holiday time it was difficult. However there was a doctor on duty at the local hospital. As he didn't know the city very well he was chauffer driven from the hospital. The child's temperature was very high and he prescribed two lots of tablets and medicine, and was sitting in the living room writing out the prescription.

I noticed how many items were being written and as I didn't have any money was feeling very embarrassed.

I had to tell him and he looked at me very surprised, saying, "This child has to have this medicine, get your coat and come with me to the hospital."

I called my neighbour Stella to look after the children until I got back, got into the car with the doctor and chauffer arriving at the hospital where he took me to the dispensary and got the different medication for me, writing the instructions on each and promising he would call again tomorrow also offering to get me a taxi home. This I refused as pride stood in the way. I thanked him and said, "It's all downhill home, although it was at least 2 miles to walk.

Next day he did call and Billy was a little better. He stood at the door talking with me, before leaving he asked why I was in such poor circumstances as I had crossed his mind several times since yesterday and he said, "You won't be charged for these visits." I explained my husband was working in England and the money wasn't coming regularly. He remarked, "My goodness, one half of the world doesn't know the other half exist do they?" Billy thankfully recovered.

Now back to the idea of looking for work myself, I applied to where I first worked when I was 15. My foreman was still there. As I explained my situation, on compassionate grounds he had to sort of create a job for me, as they didn't employ married women.

It was a 3 mile walk to work and back but I was so grateful and prepared to give it a go. So I went to see my old lady Peg, and she was delighted to move in with us. I made the single room comfortable for her and the children loved the idea of the granny figure. She loved her cigarettes and fitted in so well.

Annie was 12 months old then and Peg loved the idea of looking after the baby. Things were working out quite well, 4 of the children were at school so it was only the baby during the day, and they would all be home for lunch as the school was close by.

I had to get organised and leave all their clothes out for school at night, and prepare Annie's feeds until Peg got used to the routine.

I had an early start in the mornings from the house.It was an hours walk so I left at 6:50 a.m. to clock in for 8 a.m. Sometimes I was lucky enough to get a lift. After awhile I was finding the job too demanding and I didn't feel good in myself. I felt tired and my side ached, but the money had been a big help in sorting myself out.

Peg stayed on with us, she did lots of washing for me and we looked after her. Mary and herself were great pals, she developed a leg ulcer and attending the clinic with that.

Andy arrived home again on his second visit and he was only home a few days when I got very sick. Mammy visited me and called the doctor. I was hospitalized straight away with an enlarged kidney, explaining my tiredness and pain for some weeks previous. The surgeon asked Andy to sign a form in case I needed an operation during the night, and he did that.

The following morning however the surgeon decided not to remove the kidney if it could be avoided so I was kept under observation for 10 days with complete bed rest. The day I was to be released from hospital arrived, but instructed that I would have to return if the pain ever came back.

I was surprised how weak I was on getting up. I 'phoned my friend Noeleen and asked if she could come and collect me. She decided to call up to the house and ask Andy if he would get a taxi to take me home. His answer to her was, "Indeed I won't, she can walk." And walk I did, holding Noeleen's arm and the wall for the 2 mile journey, eventually reaching home safely.

The children were delighted to see me and my mother-in-law had been down every day to look after the children and cook. I was home a few days when I found a letter, addressed to Gwen Thomas, Andy was in the bathroom, his suit jacket hanging on the side of the kitchen door and this letter sticking up in his pocket.

I removed it on impulse. When he came out of the bathroom I asked for an explanation he demanded the letter back, I refused, pushing it down the top of my dress, but he cornered me in the hall.

Joseph, Mags, and Billy were outside in the street playing, Annie was sleeping in her pram, unfortunately Mary was around me as usual, and got between us in the hall, pushing him away, and kicking, shouting, "Leave mammy alone!"

Getting away from him and managed to hold on to the letter. The window in the living room opened out, he had a tight grip of my arm and my cardigan was undone, so I jumped out the window, leaving my cardigan in his hand and ran down the road to my friend Noeleen.

So frightened, I was oblivious to neighbours or what they might think, and giving the precious letter to my friend to mind, I made my way home to mammy, and daddy was just on his way in from work. I was very upset and trying to explain what happened when Andy knocked at the door. I couldn't believe he had actually followed me. He wanted that letter back at all costs.

Daddy opened the door and invited him in and taking him by his neck tie pushed Andy in to the armchair very roughly. Daddy was a big man so I did not know what to expect, mammy busied herself with getting the dinner in the kitchen and I joined her.

I could hear daddy's voice raised in anger, "What's your game boy? You got my daughter pure clean and decent at 18 years of age and made little of her for some woman in England, not to mention my grandchildren. I have news for you now, Brigid is going over to her sister in England for a rest, and you can look after your children for a few months, see how you will like that."

Clutching my dress in my hand in the kitchen listening to this drama taking place, (secretly delighted I was at last getting some support) then daddy came out to me and said, "Will you go love? I'll get your fare." I replied, "No, I can't leave the children." He said, "Whatever you want."

Andy was very quiet during all this, like all bullies when challenged. Daddy continued to verbally abuse him and pushed him around a bit, but didn't actually strike him. I could hear Andy say, "That's enough, sir." Mammy said nothing at all. I left for home to make sure the children were okay and he followed me down, packed his bags, and left for England early the next morning.

I still had the letter; strangely enough he had not filled in her postal address. I often wondered if he meant me to find that letter. The contents were how much he missed her, how he had been in the dog house since he came home, becoming very intimate, and a bit sickening to read really and that he had indeed asked me for a divorce on incompatibility of character.

At this time we had a parish Priest in the city I only remember as Father Shaun, whom Andy knew pretty well, as he was involved in the unions during the industrial strikes. The first few days of Andy's visit he went so far as to send me down to see him, and I was very curious as to what the Priest's opinion of our situation would be.

I got Annie ready in her pram and made my way to the presbytery, and as I was walking along on the pavement there was Father Shaun coming towards me, using a long black umbrella as a walking stick. I recall thinking, 'It must be going to rain.' I approached him, introducing myself and asking if he knew my husband. Indeed he did. Then I told him the story of how I had 5 children and Andy wanted a divorce to marry a woman in England, and that Andy had actually sent me to see him.

Father Shaun just looked at Annie in the pram and remarked, "My goodness, Andy must be a very hard man, but where is your Irish pluck?

Give him nothing, make him rear his children, and tell him to come and see me if he wants to, I certainly won't be visiting him." Later I told Andy what the Priest had said, but he was quite unmoved.

Following all the drama with the letter and his money arriving very irregularly, Andy's eldest brother called to see me one day, and offered me the fare to travel to England, which was 30 shillings, to find out what was going on. I could see a probation officer in England and get something sorted out about maintenance. His wife gave me a coat, I remember it was red with a fur collar, as I didn't have a coat good enough to travel in.

Andy's mother moved in to look after the children, she only lived a few streets away and she was so upset about all this, especially the effect it was having on the children. But she was his mother and hoping this would all sort itself out and she would say, "He will be on his knees to you yet."

I got myself ready for the trip to England though I hated travelling and nervous, never being out of Ireland before. I was 30 and the UK sounded like one of those far away places. I had Andy's address and of course he was not expecting me. I was sick on both the boat and train.

Amazed at all the activity so early in the morning, and all the different accents around me, it seemed like a different world. Now reality was setting in, I was actually on my way to where he lived, and face him in a strange country.

I noticed two nuns reading their office on the train and approached them, convinced they would have great influence with the Man Above, and explaining my circumstances that my husband was not expecting me, I had come over from Ireland and was nervous, I asked them to pray for me. They promised me they would and told me to say, "Sacred heart of Jesus, I place all my trust in you," until I reached my destination.

I kept repeating the prayer until I reached the address where I just stood and looked at the house, and wasn't afraid any more.

It was early morning time, I knocked on the door, Mr. Roache opened the door. I asked if Andy was in, explaining that I was his wife. He was embarrassed to tell me he wasn't home and called upstairs to his wife Betty to come down. It happened that Andy had not come home the night before. They were nice people and invited me in and cooked breakfast for me.

They were expecting him back soon to change into his working clothes, and sure enough he did come in by the back door and was very surprised to see me sitting at the table, and asked me what I was doing there. I replied, "To get some money from you to keep your children."

Making some sarcastic comment, he got ready and left for work, saying, "I will see you when I get back this evening," emphasizing the 'you'.

Explaining to Mrs Roache I was now desperate with 5 children to keep and no money coming for some weeks, and forced to make the journey to England, she was sympathetic and suggested I rested after the journey. I was tired and stressed, I thanked her and went upstairs, putting my small bag in the bedroom, had a wash and going back to the bedroom I suddenly felt so depressed and alone, I knelt by the side of the bed and prayed, "Dear mother of God, help me now to see this through. Don't let me go back without having sorted something out."

Just then a voice from downstairs called out, "Brigid are you in bed?" Getting up I went to the door. It was Betty Roache, asking if I could come down as they would like a word with me. When I went downstairs she told me Andy had been having an affair for some time and they had now decided upon meeting me that I was much too good for Andy, and offered me this girl's address, but bound me to secrecy as to where I got my information. I promised I would never divulge that and I never did.

The address of this girl now in my possession and following instructions for bus routes, it seemed a long way because I was tired from travelling.

But only maybe an hour's bus ride, and walking for a while before I reached the address- it was a long narrow street, my attention was drawn to two girls sitting on a window ledge, chatting. I approached one of them, asking if they knew where Gwen Thomas lived. She replied, "I'm Gwen Thomas."

She was tall and blonde, about my own age, and attractive in a brassy way. I said, "Can I speak to you privately?" She turned to her friend saying, "I'll see you later," and then asked me into a little parlour off the hallway of her house. I kept looking at her and said, "Have you no idea who I am?" In a nice English accent she replied, "No I don't know you, but I do recognise the Irish accent."

I said, "In that case I have a shock for you. Are you Andy Ryan's girlfriend?! She replied, "Yes I am." I said, "Sorry, but I am his wife," and opened my hand bag and produced a photograph of the 5 children. "And those are his 5 children." Her reaction was shock and I believed her. She said, "I never knew he was a married man, how could I? He never had any cares or worries, and when I wrote to him I believed I was writing to his sister's address. He slept here to decorate this house and asked me to get engaged."

At the time I was wearing the neck chain he had given me, and she was wearing an identical one he had given her. She then added, "Do you mind if I don't tell Dad?" I said, "I'm afraid I do. I want you to tell your father and I would like you to do it now."

She reluctantly called her father from the kitchen. He was a small, pleasant man using a stick. She introduced me saying, "Dad, this is the wife of Andy that I have been going about with, and she has five children." He shook hands with me saying, "I'm pleased to meet you, but I'm very sorry for your trouble." Her sister Mary then joined us adding, "I never liked that man, his guts were yellow the first day I saw him."

THE CONFRONTATION

It was then decided the three of us would go to his digs and meet him when he returned from work; only sheer willpower was keeping me going. Arriving at his digs at 5:30 p.m. he came in the back door while we were sitting in the living room with his landlady. Her husband went into the kitchen to tell him his wife, and Gwen Thomas and sister were waiting for him. When he got himself together he came in to meet us.

Gwen said, "Andy why didn't you tell me you were a married man?" He replied, "Because I couldn't give you up." Fiery little Mary then had her say and advised him to turn around, look at his wife, and consider his little ones, adding he wasn't fit to wipe my boots. And what about my sister, what about my dad's feelings? How did you sleep at night?

Then she struck him several times in the face with a pair of leather gloves she was carrying. Her opinion of him came tumbling out, and all he could say was, "That's enough Mary." They both then left and he followed after them. I don't know how I felt, just weary and shocked, it was almost too much to take in.

I sat talking with Betty and Tom. They gave me the address of a probation officer to see before going back home. Then about 10:30 p.m. that night there was a knock on the door - it was Andy. I said, "What do you want?" "Just to explain, I had to say all I said as she has money belonging to me, and I have to get it back'. I told him, "Please go away, and meet me in the probation officers office at 10:30 a.m. in the morning." And this he did.

Morning arrived. We both sat across the table, facing the probation officer. I explained why I was there and our problem, he listened and then asked Andy what he intended doing about his family responsibilities. In response, Andy agreed to increase the maintenance and eventually find us a home in England. The officer explained to me, "There is not a lot I can do to insure this man keeps his promise.

❋

I can't put an order on him as he says he is moving out of the city. But if he doesn't keep his word, frankly he is not worth his salt."

We both left the office and I returned home to Ireland next morning. I understood from Andy that he was moving nearer London. Travelling back home, I was going over all that had happened in my mind, deciding at least I knew where I stood. I didn't believe for a minute my maintenance would increase or that he would find us a home in England.

Andy had responded due to the fact that he was found out, knowing that I would be relating the story when I got home. Neither did I believe that she was the love of his life, she was a diversion and available. He enjoyed living like a single man and he was making the most of that opportunity.

So I had some serious thinking to do about our future - that looked bleak to say the least.

As I expected, I didn't hear from him for a few weeks after coming back home, then no address, just the telegram and the same amount of money as before and often missing a week. Relating the story to his family they were helpless anyway, and I was again calling to the presbytery collecting milk and food vouchers from the Priest, and my little corner shop continued to give me credit.

After giving it a lot of thought I decided to make another trip to England to Andy's old address, his mother again moving in to take care of the children for a week. I called to his old address but he had gone from there and was now staying with a Mrs. Power. I eventually found out he was back with Gwen again so I called to her home. The door was opened by her father, it was midday and he said, "Don't tell me this is still going on?"

He handed me a £5 note and said, "Go and get yourself something to eat and come back at 5 p.m. when she is home from work. I said, "I can't accept this money," but he insisted saying, "She is taking your share."

I accepted it and went and got myself a meal and returned to her house, as arranged. I was confronting a different woman, when challenged by her father she said, "He is not keeping me dad. I'm working for my keep," and invited me to wait while she got ready for her 7p.m. date.

I had no choice but to do this, so we boarded the bus together she paid my fair but there was no conversation between us. After a short bus ride we got off and walked along the pathway, where Andy stood at a corner near a pub.

Feeling very nervous I stood my ground and very much at a disadvantage when he asked me, what I wanted.

I replied, "An explanation at least. Remember you do have 5 children in Ireland. Maybe you would choose this woman or them."

He answered me saying, "One thing is certain, I don't want you." I had a handbag in my hand I raised it and struck him in the mouth. I just couldn't speak I felt so indignant, my self esteem taking a dive. Both of them left and went in to the pub near by.

I honestly don't know how I got back to Mrs Roache's house - I was staying at his previous digs. I was trembling and felt my knees getting weak, shock I suppose. Reaching the house I was in a state of collapse and they sat me down and kept rubbing my hands, and gave me whiskey to drink. I still couldn't speak, words wouldn't come. A dog kept whining outside the back door. Eventually I poured it all out to Mr and Mrs Roache and he remarked, "If this gets known at his job, the men will refuse to work with him."

I stayed on for a few more days and again returned home, trying to get myself together.

DECISION TIME

Shortly after this my younger sister came home from Bedfordshire on holiday and suggested I join her in England with the children and start a new life. There certainly was no future, or prospects in Ireland for me. Daddy didn't think it was a good idea, but in the end it was my decision.

Peg was a great comfort in a way, always there, but also a responsibility, and the children were very fond of her, I don't think she really grasped the situation and all she would say is, "God help us, it's terrible ma'am. I hope you won't all go to England." I knew she would miss us so much and then she would be facing an old folks home which was arranged for her before we left.

There was a lot of money owing on my furniture and I was contemplating selling all the furniture to get our fares together, as low key as possible. Then when I got to England and sorted out my life I could send monthly money to my friend Noeleen, to pay off my debt, as she had an account at the same store herself.

My sister returned to Bedfordshire and we kept in touch I still had no address for Andy as he had moved digs yet again, but I found a letter in the house of a friend of his that I knew he would be in touch with, so I kept that safely in case I needed it. The money came as irregularly as before.

I then made a third trip to England for a week and my sister and myself made several inquiries about accommodation in Bedfordshire, but it was very difficult, and we gave up in the end. I went to see the local parish Priest, a Father Rueman, and told my story. He gave me a letter for a catholic boarding school close by.

I was interviewed by the Reverend Mother, who was French. She agreed to take the children temporarily for£5 per week while I was looking for accommodation or hopefully a home for us. There were quite a few boarders and a few Irish nuns.

❈

I then saw the manager of the hostel where my sister worked as a receptionist and a job was arranged for me cleaning the chalets at £4 a week plus board and lodgings. All that done I went back home once again and explained to the children what I was doing and all about the convent.

Andy's mother was upset and had mixed feelings about it but secretly I think she believed I had no option. Daddy was completely against it, he hated any of us going to England. Mam however, did think it was the only way forward.

Then I wrote a letter of petition to our Lady of Perpetual Succour and dropped it into the petition box in our local church, telling her we were leaving and asking for her protection and intercession. Looking up at her statue I said, "Dear mother of God, its all in there." On leaving, at the end of the church I looked back at her, and cried.

Selling my furniture was easy really as it was in nice condition and it was collected at night. I paid my grocery bill at the little corner shop, also £5 I owed my doctor. I arranged with Noeleen to explain at the furniture store my situation and that I would eventually get around to paying off my bill. She was very reliable and supportive and we promised to keep in touch.

I had lovely neighbours, too numerous to mention, and Priests from our local church with whom I had always kept in touch. Now I was getting all the children bathed and clothes packed. The furniture now all sold, Noeleen took my key to hand back to the corporation.

LEAVING IRELAND FOR BEDFORDSHIRE, 1956

As we climbed into the taxi that evening, I had 5 children, 5 cases and £5.

We were then saying goodbye to neighbours and friends, trying to reassure the children, saying how nice the convent was and it would only be for a little while, and that I would be working quite near them and take them out every day and then we would get another house in England.

Mammy and daddy were at the station to say goodbye. Daddy was convinced I wouldn't be long gone before I was back, it was very sad saying goodbye. The journey was bothering me as I was a bad traveller and I knew I must be strong for this journey, I must keep going for the children as none of them had ever travelled before.

I didn't know how they were going to be. The train puffed its way out of the station along the track, with only the river and quayside in view, lights in the shop windows reflecting in the water, leaving all that was familiar and wondering what lay ahead.

It was a rough crossing and I just wished I could die and I did the worst thing I could do and stayed up on deck to get some air. The children were all sick and a lady sitting close by kept repeating, "Pretend you're on a seesaw," meaning well of course, but making us all feel worse.

Annie was in my arms all the time and slept most of the way. The journey seemed endless but we finally arrived at the convent. Reverend Mother was of stout build. It was morning time as she came down this long polished corridor to meet us. I had Annie in my arms and the cases and children gathered around me. Reverend Mother put her arms out and said, "Here she comes, with her home in her bags." Her words still ringing in my ears, I handed Annie over first and I was praying, "Please God, help me to let them go."

It was the hardest thing I ever did in my life. Billy was very quiet; he was the reserved one and didn't show emotion, especially seeing the nuns' habits, so different from home. I knew they were very scared but there was no going back now. I remember thinking, 'If I can face this. I can face anything." And I was only going down the road from them. Joseph &

Mary were holding onto me, my heart was breaking. This was the crunch. A few more nuns then joined us, making a fuss of Annie, and they were all given sweets and a meal was prepared for us.

We had our breakfast in the dining room a lot of boarders were still at the table and Mags, the friendly one, joined them and we were shown the dormitories and lockers beside the beds. Joseph wasn't impressed at all as they didn't keep boys over ten and he was only to be there temporarily. He had a room on his own, which I knew he wouldn't like, after all the company at home.

He was at an impressionable age and didn't want me to leave him. But I couldn't take him to the hostel with me as he wasn't 16.

The others had each other, and Joseph was very attached to me anyway. Eventually I had to go and get myself settled in at the hostel to start work next morning. I knew at least they were safe and warm and being fed, with clean beds, and going out to school. As this was only a boarding home visits were not restricted, so I could see them any time after they got in from school.

My sister was waiting for me at the hostel. She was on duty at reception and took me to the manager and got me settled in. The chalets were small and it was a big hostel with lots of Polish and Hungarian immigrants. My job cleaning the chalets was 9 to 4 with free board and £4 per week. Before leaving home I had written to Andy's friend, Hayden in

Warwickshire, simply saying, "Will you please inform Andy that we have now left Ireland and to forward my maintenance to Bedford General P.O. Beds. England." A shock for him, no doubt. The very last thing I did was to post that letter.

There were also lots of Irish and Welsh people in the hostel, a time of high immigration (1956). Breakfast next morning was in a large dining hall. As I waited for my sister to call me, I sat on the side of the bed, looking out the small window at lots of green fields and trees. Men were emerging from their chalets for their days work. Imagine I was actually in another country!   .

Then my mind was on the children, wondering how they felt this morning, so many thoughts racing through my mind. A knock on the door brought me back to reality. It was my sister. We both made our way to the dining hall and joined the queue, tray in hand, as breakfast was served from big containers. Food was plentiful. Most of the girls in the kitchen were Irish.

Then the housekeeper showed me the block of chalets, they were quite basic, and allotted to me 20 in each section. My job was making beds and cleaning sinks and floors, changing of beds once a week and preparing laundry..

Finishing early the next day I made my way to the convent and couldn't get there fast enough, wondering how the children had settled in. They were all in the grounds playing, and came running to meet me chanting, "It's mammy, it's mammy!"

I had brought sweets for them, however a nun spotted me and took the sweets saying, "Not before tea. These will be kept for them until after the meal." One nun had Annie by the hand - she was adapting better than I expected, and loving the attention as she was the youngest boarder.

Joseph was insisting he wasn't going to stay as he was in a room on his own and was frightened and kept saying, "I want to be with you." There was no consoling him at all. Billy was standing in the background a bit, not saying much. Mags and Mary were very much together, and exploring their new surroundings. The convent had lovely grounds lots of space fields and trees, that reminded me of Ireland.

I was telling them to look after Billy as he was shy and I hoped he would find a new little friend. Annie was content as long as she had a Mars Bar in her hand. Such different little personalities, but they were a clannish bunch really. Though Billy always had a disapproving look for Annie, and he used to say, "I don't like her." I'm sure it was the age gap. Strangely enough she loved him and it intrigued me as he could not get far enough away from her.

Now I was in England my mind was working and I had great hopes for us.

My sister Una was 22 then and going out with a Hungarian, who had just emigrated to the States, with Una to follow later when he settled. Una was a very popular and generous girl and enjoyed having us in Bedfordshire and I got to know a lot of her friends. She and I would take the children out at weekends for walks; they enjoyed their lemonade and biscuits and took the sweets back with them.

I had to apply myself to my job and concentrate on what I had to do. I was conscientious and things had to be done properly, which helped to keep my mind off the children.

Billy, and Mags were very close so she would mind him. Mary would do her best to settle just to please me. Joseph was still very unhappy as time went on, so I used to go up and take him down to the hostel with me for a few hours and try and convince him we would all be together soon. But he was making himself unpopular with the nuns because he was nervous. When in his room, he would stuff the key holes, in case they locked him in, and that was not acceptable to the discipline of the convent. Now this was a big problem.

Una and I were looking around for a flat, mobile home, anything, so that we could all be together, but nobody was interested in giving accommodation to a girl on her own with 5 children, just arrived from Ireland with no income.

※

A few weeks went by and Andy had received my letter written before I left home, informing him of my move to England, which was a big shock for him as I was soon to find out. We were in a small village like town with a nice church, and the hostel being the main accommodation apart from two hotels, and the G.P.O. Letchworth was not too far away, about an hours journey. Obviously Andy would assume the hostel was the place to find me, with the convent just up the road.

One day I was working in one of my chalets, the occupant was an Irish woman and she was sitting on the side of her bed chatting to me. The door was slightly open. Una was busy at reception, and couldn't leave her post to warn me.

Suddenly I heard the footsteps along the corridor, -that determined walk so familiar to me, getting nearer. The only door open was pushed in with his foot, and then face to face - he was glaring at me now saying, "And what have you done with my children?"

Gathering my thoughts very quickly and with an amused smile I replied, "Well that's rich coming from you." At that time no maintenance had been received for 3 to 4 weeks and only with a little help from my sister, who didn't have a lot, we managed to pay the £5 weekly fee to the convent.

My sister had by now contacted the manager and asked him to call the police to have Andy removed, but that couldn't be done as it was a domestic dispute. Una was raging at him. Then of course he had to be told where the children were.

He did go to the convent but the children were at school, except Annie. He came back to the hostel in an aggressive mood and shouted, "How dare you come to England and put my children in to a convent?!"

I still had no address for him and could only contact him through a friend. Of course he had no answer to questions thrown at him by my sister.

However before he left, Una asked him to leave his address and 'phone number as we were having big problems with Joseph and finding suitable accommodation. He did leave his 'phone number.

Soon after this Reverend Mother sent for me, concerned about Joseph; he was fretting and wasn't eating, and because of his age shouldn't be there anyway. I took him back to the hostel with me had a word with the manager who allowed me to keep him with me for just that night as rules at the hostel were strict and 16 was the minimum age he had to be to stay there as a resident. Five years to go.

Una and myself discussed our situation and she decided to 'phone Andy at the hostel in Warwickshire, informing him I had to take Joseph out of the convent.

She told him that I would be in Warwickshire the next day as Joseph could not remain with me. His answer was, "Tell her not to come, I won't be here." She replied, "You'd just better be," and she meant business. I got off work indefinitely and took Joseph by train to Warwickshire. I had 3 shillings in my pocket.

I arrived at the hostel about midday, a large scattered building and we went to reception, where there were two Irish girls on duty. I asked for Andy Ryan, explaining I was his wife and this was his little boy. A look passed between them. They were very polite helpful girls but were sorry to tell me he was not there and had booked out the night before, but if I would like to go to one of the chalets, a friend of Andy's lived there with her husband and they may be able to help me.

I thanked them and proceeded to the address given. The door was opened by her husband. After announcing who I was and introducing Joseph, he invited us in. They had married quarters. He told me that Pauline had gone shopping and would soon be back. He kindly made some tea for us.

Soon Pauline arrived back, surprised to see two visitors awaiting her. He informed her who we were and I noticed the look of amazement on her face, as if she couldn't take it in. Getting herself together she related the story. Andy had been living in married quarters with Gwen Thomas for some time and he had left that weekend taking her with him. He would be back at the hostel Sunday night, no doubt leaving his cares behind, knowing I was on my way to Warwickshire.

Andy was then working in an abattoir in Warwick. Pauline decided she would slip a note under his door asking him to come straight to her room on returning, which she expected to be late Sunday night. In the meantime I stayed there, sharing Pauline's bed, her husband doubled up with his friend next door and a make shift bed was made for Joseph on the floor.

There were community bathrooms and toilets on the block and strict rules so we all had to be very discreet. Joseph was delighted to be with me and excited about the whole thing.

On his return, needless to say Andy did not call at Pauline's, so instead she went to see him and read him the Riot Act. He just listened and said, "Yes, Brigid was a good wife and mother, but I don't want her now." Pauline replied, "Too bad, she is here now with your son and four more children in a convent, with no place to live and no money, so you'd better get married quarters and I will get Brigid a job here," slamming the door, she left.

He called to see me on his return from work that Monday, not pleased at all now with the situation he found himself in now we were on his doorstep. I knew I had to swallow my pride and play along. as I was determined to find a home in England and get the children out of the convent. He agreed, "Yes I will get married quarters, But I will make it so hard for you, you'll have to go." And he did make it hard.

I went to the parish Priest and explained our circumstances. I found going over and over the situation was draining, but I felt the sharing and the fact I was doing something was helpful. He found me a Catholic foster home for Joseph on a temporary basis, at 30 shillings a week.

Joseph was soon attending school and would come down and see me every evening at the hostel, this little boy running around the grounds was attracting attention; as a chatty likeable boy who got on well with grown ups, he did well for pocket money on Friday nights.

I had now started work at Warwick Hostel with the same wages and conditions. Una was often calling the convent in

Bedfordshire and I would chat to the children on the 'phone. I arranged to visit most weekends and sleep at the convent, giving me more time to take them out.

Reassuring them we would soon have a new house and it would work out okay, they settled well there, but there were always tears when I was leaving, which was distressing.

I was earning £4.50 weekly now and that helped, 10 shillings extra meant a lot then. I would depend on my sister to visit the children and bring them little treats. She was fond of them, however her plans were to marry and emigrate. We would all miss her when she left for the States.

I became friendly with the assistant housekeeper at the hostel, a Mayo girl, Mary O'Hara she was very helpful and found Joseph very amusing. Her boy friend Jim gave Joseph a push bike and took him out when he was free at weekends.

Andy was very difficult to live with. We had a 3ft bed, which I slept on the edge of. He went away most week-ends. He did pay the fee of £5 per week to the convent and sometimes he paid Joseph's 30 shillings, if not I did. But we had both gone to the Council House and applied for housing, on the grounds that the children were in a convent and we were all separated.

With the influence of the Priest and doctor we were being considered a priority case, which was a big step forward and more than I had dreamed of.

Housed with the children, I would be more in control of my life.

Andy was still pushing for divorce and accompanied me one evening to see the Priest. Sitting in the church in front of the altar with the Priest sitting with us, he actually told him that he wanted a divorce. The Priest advised him to go out to the church porch and get details of Catholic counselling from a leaflet displayed there.

As we were leaving the seat the Priest pushed Andy aside and said, "You just want to be off, don't you?" I think it was that same evening that Andy said to Joseph, "You're old enough now boy to know I will be leaving." The child just looked up at him and said, "How could you daddy?" Joseph was then aged 12 years.

Andy didn't get very far with the Priest who made it clear to him he had something better to be doing with his time than listening to a load of rubbish.

Most of Andy's friends were Welsh. At the hostel they were all aware of the situation and made a fuss of Joseph and myself, especially at lunch time; in the dining hall they would carry my tray to the table and chat. They thought it was all very sad as of course they had all been introduced to Gwen Thomas before our arrival on the scene. They flattered me too saying, "Why would any man want to leave a woman like you with five children?" I'm sure their opinion of him had dropped considerably, but no one could interfere.

On one particular week-end Andy said, "This evening I must go and see Gwen as she has £150 belonging to me and I want it back now. I will need it when we get the house, she has two brothers so I don't know what might happen. If I'm not back on Sunday night, I want you to come down."

He wrote Gwen's sister's address, where she was staying, on a Woodbine packet and he took off. I was working that Saturday morning and talking to Mary O'Hara, my friend whom I confided in. Sunday night came and he had not returned, then the drama began. I went to see Mary before starting work Monday morning explained that he had not yet returned so between us we decided I should travel to the address he gave me. I wondered what situation I would find there.

I had very little money with me, a few shillings at most. Arriving at the address, her sister Mary opened the door. I asked for Gwen, she came out and looking at me she said, "If you are looking for Andy he is in Rugby."

I asked her if she would recognise his handwriting. She replied, "I ought to." I showed her the woodbine packet saying, "He told me you had £150 belonging to him and he had come to collect it and asked me to come to this address in case anything had gone wrong.

I must correct you on one thing though. Andy is not in Rugby. He is in fact living with me in Warwick and we are waiting for a council house." Replying she said, "Well you go back and tell him if I did have £150 belonging to him he would not get it back."

I returned that day. My ticket only took me to Birmingham and it was dark, almost 9:30 at night. There was a line of taxis outside the station. I approached one of the drivers asked him if he would take me to Warwick and I would pay him when I got home. I knew I could approach Mary O'Hara for the money. He hesitated and said, "I really must have some sort of security." I was wearing a ring Una had given me so I offered him the ring. He gave me a receipt, stating the ring was to be returned on payment for the taxi, which I promised to send on.

Andy was in bed asleep. I woke him of course and had to listen to a load of rubbish and excuses but he knew he was in trouble with Gwen Thomas for sure.

I saw Mary next morning and she lent me 30 shillings for my ring to be returned, which I received by return post shortly after.

Through all the injustice I trusted in God who had suffered much injustice himself. I did not have time to think too deeply, everything was happening so quickly. The day to day routine continued. My sister's boyfriend returned from the States; they married in Bedfordshire then both left for the U.S.A. I missed Una as we were both in close contact about the children as she had visited as often as she could and took them out.

I kept pursuing the council house and continued to work at the hostel, and kept in touch with home which was very close to my heart. I knew they were all concerned for us. I had to move forward now and think of the children. After 18 months we were allotted a council house in Warwickshire for rent of £3 per week.

It was a large 5 bedroom house with sitting room, dining room, kitchen and pantry, a lovely long tiled hall, large back garden with apple trees and small front garden. It had been unoccupied for sometime but had been a surgeon's house at one time and was in a good area of Warwick. It was on a lovely road but busy, traffic wise. The wiring was poor and in generally bad shape, and every room needed decorating.

We were told we could have it for 5 years as that particular row of houses were to be demolished to make way for new roads, but then we would automatically be transferred to another house. I was delighted - my dream had come true. They called it the Irish Man's Pad as there was so many boarding houses around that particular area, and of course the Midlands had a lot of Irish residents.

I just couldn't believe I now had the key of a house in my hand. Imagine, I actually made it all happen! The excitement continued as I rang the children with the news.

❋

They were overjoyed, and Joseph especially, was delighted. Andy, Joseph, and myself moved in and one of Andy's Welsh friend's Bryan, rallied around. He was clever with electricity and tidied up all the wiring while I did the cleaning.

It was of course completely empty and had to be furnished. And I had to be very pleasant to Andy as I was now solely dependent upon him Fortunately there were some good auction rooms close by. I wasn't sure at all how much he was prepared to spend, but I kept bidding for all the absolute necessities: beds; table and chairs; cooker; sauce pans; radio; bed linen; blanket; an old trunk full of towels; an old tin bath full of china; wardrobes; chest of drawers; arm chairs dining room suite; pieces of carpets and old grand father clock which cost 10 shillings. I remember the total bill for all these items was £75. This was 1958. Andy thought he had spent a fortune, and kept reminding me.

When everything was arranged and the big day arrived for the children to come home, I was baking and preparing a little party with lemonade and sweets and anything else I could afford. Bryan brought some gifts of biscuits and he also went to the convent to collect the children, being one of the few friends that had a car. A few hours later and they were all back from Bedford complete with bags and baggage.

Anne was almost 3 years old then and with great excitement explored the house and garden. They had spent 18 months in the convent but at last we were all together. As the days went by they told me all their different experiences in the convent, which weren't very pleasant. It was the first time they had ever complained.

During the time the children were being cared for at the convent Reverend Mother Mamair died. There was a large picture of her hanging in the dormitory and one particular nun would stand rigid under this picture at night, obviously to frighten the children going to the toilets.

❄

Mags would always wake Billy to take with her she was so scared, Another form of punishment was if any child wet the bed, the sheet was wrapped around him and he was made to turn around several times.

Annie was only 2 ½ years and was smacked for wetting the bed but one very kind nun took Annie under her wing and eventually took her to sleep with her. It seemed to be more mental cruelty than physical. I thank God now they only spent 18 months there; some children were left there 16 years. When I asked them why they never told me this before, they said they were frightened of the nuns and that they had nowhere else to live and knew I would be upset. I was horrified.

The next move was getting them registered at school and with a doctor. It was a great feeling - I had actually made it in a different country with more opportunities a new beginning - and the children were happy. I got the 4 of them in to Catholic schools, Annie was still too young.

There was no heating in the house, just fireplaces and I had an oil heater in the dining-room. Our next door neighbour called in to welcome us and offered me two single beds and some rugs and electric fire. I was delighted to get them. It was a big house to furnish but gradually I got it all together. There was some old carpet on the stairs and lino on the bedrooms and bathroom so it was mop and bucket to clean those up Hall kitchen and pantry were tiled and given a good scrub and they were perfect. The bedrooms were huge.

My idea was to take in lodgers as there were lots of Irish men on the buildings in the Midlands, and following the war no bother to get lodgers. From time to time you saw jumble sales advertised in church halls only a bus ride away. I would dress down with a scarf on my head to disguise myself in case I ran into neighbours. I picked up lots of bargains in bed linen and children's clothes and enjoyed washing and ironing them. I had a twin tub Hoover washing machine - another bargain from the auction rooms.

❋

My first lodger was an Irish man from our home town, an old school pal of Andy's and he was to be with us for 12 years. He shared a bedroom with Joseph, now aged 14 years, and they were great pals. Pat was one of the family and had all his meals with us. He called all the girls, "His queens."

Every Friday night Pat would always have a bag of sweets in his pocket for Annie, being the youngest she was his pet. Mags amused him Being the devil may care, Mary was the caring one, always helping out even at an early age - a very special child.

Billy still tended to have a go at Annie, never missing an opportunity. This amused Pat a great deal he used to say, "Lord God that young fellow has an awful down on her." But Annie was always trying to please him. Joseph was the bossy boots and went off to the market for me on a Friday with his push bike to get my fruit and vegetables.

Andy worked in an abattoir in the town and earned good wages. I was getting £12 a week then. But his old lifestyle continued and he was out every evening to his clubs and dance halls. If the children needed school uniforms or plimsoles for P.E. it was always, "Ask your mother, she's getting the wages." He constantly reminded me of what the furniture cost him for the house.

I got a job on the evening shift in an electrical factory 7 A.M. – 10 A.M. doing component wiring for radio and TV to earn extra money for furniture, to fulfil my plan. By this time I was feeling very tired and was suffering from anxiety. I was on medication for that and I really couldn't afford to be sick now. I knew it was normal reaction in the circumstances. Annie was coming up for school age and would be soon attending the infants class.

I could eventually manage to take about 7 lodgers, that included Pat, having a large dining room and sitting room, kitchen and pantry downstairs. I could turn the sitting room into a bedroom to take 2 single beds and 4 beds in the large back room upstairs.

❋

Andy was still restless and unpredictable, making any excuse to get away. Some weekends he would say a motor show was on, though he was a man that never showed any interest in cars. I guessed something was going on. He had no interest in the children's schooling.

I wanted to get a gas fire in the kitchen it meant hire purchase, but no, he wouldn't sign the form. I forged his signature and got it anyway. He was short tempered and was likely to throw his dinner around the walls. Or he would open his lunch to see what I put in his sandwiches and if he didn't like what I gave him he would squeeze it in his fist until it bulged through his fingers and walk out.

I gave him plenty of rope because now I had a house and could make a living I didn't have to take any nonsense. However mental cruelty is almost impossible to prove, so I had to have concrete evidence of adultery to get a legal separation.

My sister Lena often paid a visit; she had 2 children then and it was only a couple of hours journey, My mother and mother in law also came for visits to see our new house and stayed a few weeks at a time.

Andy's brother and sister in law came over from Ireland with their son Shaun for a week, during which time Shaun stood in the sink in the bathroom to look out the window and cracked the sink. His mother Ann went running upstairs shouting at him, "The first time you ever saw a bathroom in your life you had to break the sink!" She was nearly in tears saying, "Now I'll have to buy a sink for Brigid before I go back home." I assured her she would not.

That year we had a great crop of apples. Ann and the children would climb up the tree and picked apples and we had tarts galore for tea; Ann was also a great pastry maker. Andy's mother was especially delighted to see the children settled and happy. Mammy loved visiting England, she would help in the garden and Mary and herself were very close.

Our house was always full of the children's friends, Ruth Ward comes vividly to mind, Mag's friend in school. She would help me peel the potatoes and take every little eye out of them. At night she would likely hide under the bed when it was time to go home. Her mother, Mrs Ward, was a regular visitor.

Alan was Billy's friend. A particularly sad time was when Nigel Joseph's friend was killed in a motor bike accident. Biddy, a girl from our home town actually lived with us. She worked in the British Home Stores and later married a Belfast man. I can't even imagine now where we all slept, but we managed, and had lots of laughs.

Andy was usually on his best behaviour when we had visitors as he liked an audience, and he was very popular. They thought he was a grand fellow. He never really wanted to let go, after all he had the best part of both worlds.

I had my mind made up now I was not taking his abuse any longer. My sister Lena, on one of her visits, offered to lend me the money for a private detective to have him followed; I said I would think about it. One weekend I was feeling more tired than usual, it was evening time and I fainted. There was such a commotion. Joseph called the lady next door and she phoned the doctor. I could hear everything going on and someone asking, "Is it a heart attack?" and the doctor saying, "No her pulse is racing, she's had a nervous break down." All I could feel was a rapid pulse in my throat. I was 37 years old then.

My neighbour and the doctor helped me upstairs to bed. I recall the doctor saying to me, "You're very tired Brigid, so I will be sending you to hospital for a rest." Joseph was then 17, Mags 15, Mary 13, Billy 11, Annie 7 years old.

❋

I wasn't reacting at all, everything was mechanical. Annie had lots of blonde curly hair then and I was holding her hand, and feeling nothing. The ambulance arrived and I went to a psychiatric hospital were I was detained for 9 weeks. I had shock treatment and the after effects were awful, I kept vomiting.

I wasn't responding to that as they had hoped, so the psychiatrist asked me if I would object to Pentathol, which was known as the truth drug. I said, "I don't care, just get me better."

I was given this treatment by injection I fell asleep and a doctor sat with me. When I woke there was a nurse sitting by my bed, and I remember thinking, "Oh no, I'm not back, I can't take any more." I was just sitting around like a zombie and I was on a lot of medication. It was a dreadful experience. Following that there was medication and counselling and I was let home weekends, Friday to Sunday. I recall just sitting in the house, not noticing much, everything was so unreal.

Eventually being discharged and attending Out Patients, and a nurse calling once a week for six weeks.

My doctor was very kind and helpful, explaining it was delayed reaction to all the stress over the years and I had been very ill so recovery would be very slow. He told me to expect bad days, if I could do that it would be much easier, adding, "You are a Catholic so put your hands together and pray. You are also intelligent, another thing in your favour."

Andy doesn't come to mind at all during this bad period of my life - no doubt he was making the most of his freedom. I really don't know how the children were reacting to all this trauma as I was just in a world of my own. Mornings were the worst time of the day as I was on strong sleeping tablets and other medication. I couldn't concentrate on prayer except to repeat "Jesus help me keep hold of me".

I was gradually starting to get better when I started to get poison pen letters through the post which were cut out of newspapers and pasted onto a cornflake box, folded and put into an envelope. They read, "Your husband has been spending weekends with Mrs L Rellis of Waver Road, London - unscrupulous where men are concerned (warn your husband)."

My sister Una came over on holiday from the States and I showed her the letters; there were 3 of them, all similar. She told me take them to the police adding, "I wonder would Andy be sending them?" I froze when I first got them and it struck me could it be him, but I dismissed it from my mind almost immediately.

I was about 4 months out of hospital at this time and in the meantime my sister Lena visited me and lent me £25 to have him followed one weekend. Sure enough he was caught at a hotel booked into a double room with Gwen Thomas. I now had evidence of his adultery and a court hearing was pending for a legal separation, which I had to wait some time for.

I got legal aid and the atmosphere in the house for these waiting months was almost unbearable. Andy made his presence felt with a vengeance and all that kept me going was one day it would all be over and he would be gone. We had separate bedrooms of course, by this time. He still paid his £12 a week and was coming and going as usual.

I eventually decided to take the letters to the police and a Scottish inspector interviewed me. I explained I had received 3 of these letters and I was waiting for a court order against my husband pending a legal separation. He asked me if I had any idea who was sending them. I said, "No," and that I had recently had a breakdown.

He told me that was one reason why he would investigate these letters for me. Normally he would advise me to burn them but he was sympathetic as his sister also suffered with depression. As I was leaving he said, "Will you ask your husband to come and see me," which surprised me.

I told Andy they wanted to see him at the police station and he did go. I was in bed when he got back. He came into the bedroom and with his back to me, looking through the mirror arranging his tie to go out, he remarked, "I'm not sending them anyway." Immediately I thought, 'My God, you are. But why?'

※

Next morning I called to the station and asked to see the inspector and told him exactly what had happened when my husband got back home, He said, "Why didn't you tell me that you suspected him?" "Because I had been in a psychiatric hospital," I said, "And it was so far fetched you might think I was crazy." He replied, "Not that far fetched, these letters are intended to try and have you committed. He was questioned here and denied it, but he did not fool me at all. I think he is sending them and I've cautioned him. I don't think you will get any more, (and I never did). He said, "You think you have problems? Your husband is the one with problems." I was determined now this was not going to get to me and I would go down fighting.

SEPARATION ORDER

The day arrived for the court case; a big ordeal in 1964. Evidence was given by the private detective, and he had a solicitor and I had mine. I won the case, got custody of the children and awarded £2 a week for each child under 16, and £6 a week for myself. Andy had reasonable access.

There was a big clause that stated as we were in a Council house - which was in his name, I could leave the house with the children and they would evict him and then reinstate me. Or I could put his bags outside the door and if he tried to re-enter the house I could call the police and produce the court order.

I did ask him to leave and he said he would when he was ready. I couldn't leave with 5 children, there was no place else to go and I didn't want to subject the children to a scene if I actually put his bags out. However he stayed and on and it went into weeks. My doctor told me, "If this situation continues you will land yourself back in hospital, and the next time you may not come out so easily. I cannot advise you but I think you know what you must do."

❈

So I made my mind up, I returned home, packed his bags and put them outside the back door. Fortunately we had a side entrance to the house. I knew he would make a very dramatic departure with the goodbyes to the children, and sure enough that's what he did. He kept tapping at the kitchen window for Mary to let him in, using emotional blackmail at every opportunity.

Anyway he climbed in the kitchen window. I confronted him and said, "If you are not out of here in 15 minutes, I'm calling the police. He said his goodbyes to the children, as if he was going to America instead of up the road to the hostel. I sat down and cried with relief, I felt as if the house had been lifted off my back, it was such a big ordeal.

Still going through a bad time with depression, I kept telling myself, "Keep going."

While shopping in Warwick one day I was delighted and surprised to meet my old friend Mary. We had such a lot to talk about from home, including the time when we tried to stowaway. She had married an Irish lad and never had any children and lived just outside Warwick. Through Mary I got to know another family from home that were neighbours of hers; Mai and Tom Foley. And Mai's sister Breda had lived across the road from me in Ireland (talk about a small world). We arranged to have a get together sometime in the future as we had so much to catch up on.

I was slowly getting stronger in myself, although the depression was never very far away, but I was coping. So I decided to take a job outside the house. Since the breakdown I had finished with the evening shift work in the factory. I applied for a position as hospital psychiatric nursing assistant. Mary was already doing a nursing course in the same hospital.

❉

Annie was now 11 and capable of getting herself off to school. Joseph was now in an apprenticeship as a machine tool fitter. Billy was working as a trainee butcher. Mags was a secretary in a car factory.

Strangely enough the psychiatric nursing appealed to me and I found it interesting. Having experienced the illness myself, I thought I could be helpful to other patients. The hospital was about 8 miles outside Warwick. Mary and myself had the same uniforms.

The hospital had large grounds and we often passed each other as we were posted to different wards and this amused us. After 6 months I was invited to do an exam on my practical work and after that course I would be made up to a state mental nurse. That was 1965.

There were a lot of seriously ill patients, some of them were committed and we carried bunches of keys on a belt around our waist when working on secure wards. It was hard work, but interesting.

Mary was good on the geriatric wards. I was within 3 weeks of completing my course and going into my nurse's uniform when I gave up the nursing.

I found the journey long in the winter and hoped maybe to get similar work nearer home I would have a good reference. Mary also gave up nursing, which I thought was a pity, as she was such a caring person, I felt she would have been successful. But she soon applied for a job in the office of a local factory, and always helped out in the house in the evening.

I was catching up on a lot of housework. Pat, our lodger, was still with us and also 2 Scottish lads, and Pete my youngest lodger. One of the Scots lads emigrated to Canada. Bill stayed on and Mags and himself got very friendly and started going out together.

❋

Mary and Mags hated all the auction furniture and would scrub and polish all the furniture I bought. Mags and myself shared a double bed in the back room. We weren't long in bed one night when the bed collapsed with a big thud. It was a huge bed which meant that while the head stayed in position, the foot of the bed was on the floor. All I could do was laugh, but Mags wasn't amused at all and kept saying, "Mum, what are we going to do now, we can't stay here like this all night?"

When I was able to compose myself I suggested that maybe she would call Bill who was watching TV downstairs, and just then the bed fell with such a thud that the leg of it went through the floorboards emerging in the kitchen. Billy was sitting at the table looking up he saw the ceiling crack, shouting up to me at the bottom of the stairs he said, "Something is coming through the ceiling!" I replied, "Don't worry, it's only the leg of the bed."

Mags was by this time contemplating how she could ask Bill to help us, she was mortified. Joseph was out. I was still laughing and trying to climb out of the bed. I guess I was aged about 40 then.

In the end Mags reluctantly called Bill. He had a strong Scottish accent commenting, "You have a wee bit of a trouble here. I'll have to get something in the morning to fix it." Then he dislodged the bed from the top end and we both slept on the floor that night, much to Mag's disgust. She just could not see the funny side at all. Bill being her boyfriend added more to the horror of the situation. Bill did fix the bed the following day and we were back to normal again.

Being a very Christmasy person I loved this special time of year. It was usual to have snow, then nice warm fires while getting our decorations up. I loved the build up, and the baking of Christmas cakes and puddings. Then it was hard work. You mixed the cake with a large wooden spoon, creaming the butter and sugar, whipping the eggs with a fork.

The children, when they were young, were likely to get involved, lining the tin especially to clean out the mixing bowl after I had spooned it in to the cake tin. This they did by running their fingers around the bowl and usually ending up in a big fighting match with sticky faces and fingers.

Baking the cake was a tedious job and opening the door half way through the cooking and closing it very gently, any cold air getting into the oven would cause the fruit to drop in the cake and sink to the bottom - what a tragedy that would be with the cost of the ingredients. Usually I was lucky and it turned out successfully. I would call the children to smell it and we would all stand back and admire this beautiful cake. Next day it was wrapped well in grease proof paper and stored until almond and white iced Christmas week.

Hearing the carol singers I would lose myself for a few hours. Christmas Eve I would do my potato stuffing; plenty of finely chopped onion with mixed herb, well mashed together with the potato and a little butter and seasoning, left to get cold, then transferred into the cavity of the turkey, then stitched up and ready for the oven Christmas morning.

We always went to 9 o'clock mass which was about a miles walk. It was 10:30 by the time we got home in nice time to put the bird into the oven, ready for a late dinner. Usually I only had 2 lodgers staying for Christmas, Pat and Pete, the others, mostly Irish, loved to return home to Ireland for the festive season.

It was great having the house to ourselves. Pat enjoyed his Christmas. The Irish clubs opened up after mass and he usually came home merry. Annie knew he hated trifle after his turkey dinner and she would force Pat to swallow a spoonful. Joseph sometimes would put a tape recorder on. Pat might even give us a bar of a rebel song if he was merry enough.

This did not please Pat at all if it was played back to him but he was easy going with a dry sense of humour so he took it all in his stride. Pat's holiday time to his native land was always summer or spring, he was very patriotic.

Billy had now left school but often made a trip back home to Ireland, where he stayed mostly with his uncle and aunt their son Shaun who was his best friend. Joseph had almost finished his apprenticeship met and married an Irish girl who was a nurse in Birmingham.

Mary O'Hara had since married (my friend from the hostel days). She had one little girl, Kathleen, whom I was godmother to. They often came to see us. I would occasionally arrange to meet Mary my old friend and we would enjoy a coffee in a restaurant talking about the crazy things we did when we were 16.

Mai and Tom Foley were also visitors we enjoyed having and I would call on them from time to time. Mai was a good dressmaker and often made a dress for the girls. We had nice social evenings at Tom and Mai's house. At one particularly sad time in my life Mai's mother back in Ireland sent me a little consolation prayer I never forgot, "Take my cross and be afraid of nothing. I have weighed and measured it in the balance of love Amen."

Andy's reasonable access to the children meant he would sit outside the house in his car, usually Friday nights and they would go out and see him for 15 to 20 minutes and get their pocket money if they were lucky and he had enough change. Not having it was a favourite habit of his. And his affair with Gwen continued in a fashion never came to anything, but he was never short of a girl friend.

The money management went on. My pen and paper were out every Friday night working out the weekly bills, making sure at least these were covered, plus grocery money.

※

I was good at making bread pudding with left over stale bread apple tart, and rice puddings, all useful for dessert. I was thrifty enough and somehow always managed to make everything appear plentiful. There was a second hand gown shop in the town that sold German clothes only and it was common to see teachers, nurses, Italians, and lots of Irish waiting patiently, even in the rain, for this shop to open, especially on Fridays when new stock arrived.

I began to be an expert on designer labels and they did sell beautiful clothes. There was also nice bed linen and curtain nets, you almost became addicted, it was entertaining too. So most of my problems were solved in a remarkable way. I had to be tuned in to survive, and it kept me busy. I seemed to be always carrying bags when I wasn't working.

Mags and Bill went out together for 7 years before marrying. They had one daughter, Deborah. Mary and Dave married almost the same time and had a son Jack. Annie was the last to marry, at 18, and she also had a son called Steven. Billy had a few girlfriends but nothing serious.

As our row of houses were now due for demolishing we were offered a new house on a new estate - that was 1971. It was a nice 3 bedroom, modern house but I had a feeling this estate was going to get very rough, and we were given time to decide.

I looked around my big old house, full of memories. All that had taken place in the last 12 years; the striving to furnish it, the joy when the children came back from the convent and the lodgers that had given us so many laughs, especially Pat and Pete. But there was a disadvantage as it was a cold house. Still it had given us a new beginning.

Pat's olive oil, which was used as hair oil in winter time, turned to ice in the bottle, and the condensation inside the windows would turn into icicles, but the advantages outweighed the disadvantages.

❈

We were so central to church, markets, and schools. And this was where I became free of Andy, I was no longer in his power.

Now there was a big job ahead, I had to get rid of so much furniture, deciding to take the house in binley Grange. Being in possession of Council property I always had a chance of an exchange if the opportunity arose.

I loved old houses they are full of character.

So we prepared for the big move. Billy at this time was 21. He was in Ireland and had decided he would stay awhile, being close to the cousins, and he loved the countryside fishing and hunting - a real outdoor man.

Joseph was married with one daughter lived in Birmingham. Mags and Mary were both married now and pregnant Mags had just moved into her new house in Warwick. Mary and Dave came to live with me, waiting for their own house which Dave was renovating. Annie's wedding was planned in the near future. So there were only 4 of us now. My lodgers Pat and Pete found accommodation elsewhere.

Writing home to my parents and auntie, also Noeleen, whom I kept in touch with always, and sending on the money to pay off my furniture bill, I was getting there slowly. They all now had my forwarding address. Then we were nearly 15 years in England. Arriving at our new house, it was so nice, everything new and bright - a lot smaller of course but plenty of room for 4 of us as it happened.

Annie's weekend job was not too far from the house. I never forgot to count my blessings we had come a long way since 1956. I was still uneasy about the area and it was a long bus ride to the city centre. The surrounding houses were soon occupied with young families and lots of children so it was noisy in the evenings.

I kept watching the evening paper where you would find houses to exchange and yes, there was one anxious to get exactly where we were living.

※

I went to see the house and agreed on the exchange so in 1972 we moved back to the city centre.

The house needed improving but Mary's husband Dave was good with his hands and improved the house a lot for me. He wallpapered and painted, and once again we had a nice home.

Annie got married that year to John. Mary had a son, Jack, a lovely little boy and they were still with me. It seemed in no time at all I had 3 grandchildren. I was then aged 48, and was working as a home help.

My mother became very ill and I went back home in March 1973 to nurse her. I stayed 6 weeks as I had compassionate leave from my job. Mary and Dave were keeping the house ticking over.

I wasn't in a good position financially and it was another very stressful time in my life. Daddy had glaucoma, his sight was deteriorating and he was very difficult to manage. Mammy had stomach cancer she was now 69.

I was on day and night duty as she was very ill and it was so hard to watch her dying. Emotionally I was not up to it due to the depression which always managed to get to me.

I returned to England in early May. My sisters were visiting home on their holidays before returning to work and then continuing to 'phone home. Mammy died later that year.

Daddy lived on in the house alone, eventually going blind. I visited him when I could and kept in touch by 'phone as he couldn't read letters. He died in hospital aged 85. My sister Lena bought the family home and sold it some years later.

Settled in again at my job as a home help, all the family now had their own homes, except for Mary and Dave. I was close to Jack, he was a lovely little boy and often stood at the front door to wave me off to work. He would climb into my bed on a Sunday morning and I told him nursery stories.

❄

Joseph now had 2 girls I only got to see occasionally as they lived in Birmingham. Deborah was a lovely cute child and intelligent, but could be moody. She was my godchild, Mag's daughter.

I didn't have any social life really except to visit my old friend Mary and often we got together with Mai and Tom Foley especially when they had Irish visitors and they included me in their house parties. I always loved dancing and there were lots of places one could go but I guess I felt at a disadvantage on my own.

I got to know Sarah Campbell, a very nice lady who was a widow. She had done a lot of counselling, a very intelligent woman and on the committee of a club for divorced people. She invited me along one evening. It was a nice club with a mixed age group and I got lots of dances. However I was very much on my guard, and very choosy.

At one of these dances I noticed a man that was a little different, who stood on his own at the back of the dance hall and I guessed he was a foreigner. I wasn't surprised when he tapped me on the shoulder and said, "Like to dance madam?" It was the Vienna Waltz, which he did very well, he was a beautiful dancer. We didn't do a lot of talking and he escorted me back to my seat after the dance, bowed slightly and thanked me.

Sarah and myself always left the dance together as we didn't live far from each other. The following week I was to meet my foreigner again at another dance. He was very discreet and did introduce himself; he was Polish and a bachelor. His English wasn't good but he was an intelligent deep man, that was how I summed him up,

He had immigrated to England in 1957 and he worked as a miner and had 2 houses in Leicester. I gathered he had worked very hard to achieve the standards he now had. As the weeks went on we got to know each other a little better, as he was a regular visitor to the dances. He wondered where I had sprung from.

❀

I explained I had been separated for some years and had a family to bring up, not leaving me any opportunity to socialise. From our conversations I guessed he was a capitalist big time, and he had been in a managerial position in Poland when his country was taken over. He was very bitter about that and inclined to be arrogant. One night he asked to take me home; he had a nice sports car. My house was only a 10 minute run from the dance hall. He seemed a nice man, had a serious side to him but could also be funny.

I was now 50 and he 49. We enjoyed dancing together and each other's company. He took me to see his house in Leicester one evening, a typical bachelor home. He did a lot of his own plumbing and electrical work and liked gardening and produced most of his own vegetables. He also had a Polish lodger

Mary was curious and when I got in from the dance she asked about John and if I liked him. All the family were glad

I was getting out now and meeting people. It was helping to give me a lift and get me over the bad times of depression.

One evening I asked John into the house to meet Mary and Dave and we also later called on Joseph and Mary in Birmingham, so eventually he got to know all the family. He had nice friends, some of them German but mostly Polish.

His opinion of the Irish men amused me as he described them as being very clever men who seemed to have wives and families in Ireland and girl friends in England, and yet they got away with it.

From what I could gather from his friends John had lots of women, but they could not imagine him ever marrying. John was generous in an impulsive sort of way. We sometimes would go around the shops on Saturday.

On one of these occasions he stopped outside a jewellers and he invited me to go in and look around, asking the assistant to see some watches and bracelets, and insisting on buying me one of each saying, "You like?" I replied, "Yes, I love them, thank you." I was very proud to show Mary my gifts on arriving home.

We were by now going to the dances together and on one of these occasions we were both sitting at a small table enjoying a drink. John was sitting facing the door and he remarked to me, "My dear your ex has come in the door with a ginger lady."

And sure enough Andy strode by with his arm around his girl friend and they both sat near the stage. The next dance was John's favourite the *Vienna Waltz*. I think we were the first on the floor. I quite enjoyed dancing past him and I imagine it was a shock for Andy.

John was tall and carried himself well but was getting bald, making him look older than he was. He was a popular man in general, and attentive. I sensed he could be posses-sive. Although he was generous he was also very careful with money and more interested in investing rather than spend-ing. Although John didn't have an outstanding personality he had a sense of humour all his own.

While sitting together on another occasion at the dance a man I knew to be a good dancer approached our table and asked John if he could have this dance with me. While we were waltzing around the floor the inevitable happened, I fell and my partner fell on top of me. The dance was just finish-ing, John strode slowly across the floor and looking down at me said, "Serves you right dear. Who do you think you are, Ginger Rogers?" To say I was embarrassed would be an un-derstatement.

We were seeing each other for about 12 months when John was preparing for his regular trip to Poland. His awk-ward way of proposing was, "I would love to take you, but I could not do that unless we were married."

❋

His father was Protestant and his mother Catholic and they agreed the boys would be brought up Protestant and the girls Catholics.

A few weeks later we bought the engagement ring, I took court proceedings to divorce Andy. After talking with the parish Priest that was easy, we had been legally separated for so many years anyway, it was only a matter of form.

I was now seriously considering my position. I was working part time with a council house and the future looked bleak. The Priest was very sympathetic and understanding and made it very clear he could not give a blessing to a registry office marriage which was the only way open to me. Yes I could apply for an annulment if it could be proved Andy never took responsibility.

Asking the Priest how long that would take, he told me that in my case that would take years. "Years I didn't have years I was already 51," I said. Father, Almighty God has annulled my marriage over this table between you and me this morning, because he never did take responsibility." Surprising me, the Priest replied, "We do know a lot about you and realise you have had a rather hard and tragic life and whatever you may decide to do, keep in touch with us anyway."

My eldest son's advice was, "If you can make it right between you and God then it's right for you, but the question you must ask yourself is can you? And also remember he is of a different culture." I had related this to the Priest during our conversation and he said, "Your son gave you very good advice indeed."

John and myself never at any time considered living together and he did seem anxious that we marry before the planned holiday to Poland. Of course I did a lot of thinking, could I find happiness?

I wouldn't say I was madly in love; we got on well together and I felt we had similar moral standards. John's Letter of Freedom was sent on and the bands were displayed in the Warwick registry office.

※

We discussed a lot of things, including me giving up my council house, he was anxious I did this and I agreed.

The wedding took place in July 1976, all my family attended with some of my own close friends. John's sister and her husband came from Poland. The reception was held in the Polish Club where we first met. We moved into his semi detached house in Leicester, where there were three bedrooms, one of which the lodger occupied, whom I expected would be moving soon now that John and I had married.

We spent the first few days shopping and preparing for our holiday in Poland. His family were nice people, the language barrier was a problem, I was just getting nods of approval. The weather was usually predictable but in 1976 it rained a lot in Poland. However upon returning to England the grass was burned from the sun, it had been a real hot summer.

We settled down to married life in Leicester and it was very strange to me, after being on my own for so long. John got back to his job. We had radiators throughout the house and these were heated from a range effect stove in the living room as he was allowed coal cheap being a miner.

Now that we were married I was planning on changing a few things in the house to make it real cosy. I knew he wasn't short of money and thought would be delighted to give everything a new look and all his friends we visited were very house proud. I had ideas of a red hall with white paintwork and doors to give a welcoming look. It was a nice shaped hall but the house lacked atmosphere. The furniture was old in the sitting room and the whole house needed doing.

The first setback I had was when John paid for all the groceries and supplied my cigarettes; I was smoking at that time. We had a nice car and all my needs were taken care of. I didn't know how to handle the situation it was not something I expected and it now became embarrassing.

✳

The lodger was still in the house and this irritated me as he cooked in the kitchen. I couldn't use the kitchen when I needed to and he hardly spoke, as if he resented me being there.

John and myself shopped together for the groceries, he paid and it was, "Please let me know if you need anything." Nothing was ours, everything was his. One day I suggested we tile the kitchen as the lino was old. Begrudgingly he agreed to do this.

If I moved anything in the house when he was at work on his return he would say, "This has to go back to where it was." When I baked cakes he asked me if I thought I was feeding an army. He was not intending to ask his lodger to move out. It was becoming apparent that money was very important to John, and this man was contributing.

We were now only months married it was becoming more obvious this man was not prepared to share his life and possessions with anyone. I tried talking and discussing serious issues with him but I felt he was using the language barrier as an excuse, always saying, "I do not understand."

In plain language I told him this lodger would have to go. I had to have my kitchen to myself, I could no longer live under the strain of having to ask for everything I needed and furthermore I did not intend to as I had managed my own life for far too long to be controlled by any man again.

He said, "You are a very stupid woman. Where will you go? You have no home to go to." And he was quite amazed I was behaving like this and pointing out I brought nothing into the marriage therefore I could expect nothing if I left.

Now this was another big shock to me, we were now 4 months married in October. I knew by his attitude this man was determined, things were not going to change. I knew I could not be controlled ever again. It crossed my mind, 'What have I done to myself?' I was now confronting a complete stranger to the man I met 16 months ago.

❋

Trying to think very quickly now, I felt so embarrassed and disgusted I just wanted out of his sight. Reluctantly and feeling very ashamed and needing to be on my own, I 'phoned my son-in-law and asked him if he would come to Leicester and pick me up.

John saw me gather a few items of clothing in a bag, again saying, "You have nowhere to go." I just looked at him and said, "Don't worry about me, I'll find somewhere. What you don't seem to realise is that I would go out there on that street and break stones before I would allow you to control me." He repeated again, "I never think so you like this," in his broken English.

I said, "No John, and what did you think? That you had met a simple Irish girl who had a hard life bringing up children on her own and would be very happy with a roof over her head, housekeeping for a Polish man? Well I'm afraid you are greatly mistaken."

My son-in-law Dave pulled up outside the door and I left, wondering how I would feel explaining all this to my family and friends, and above all trying to take in how he talked me into giving up my home. How could I have been so stupid? I couldn't cry, I couldn't feel anything.

Mary was very understanding when I arrived and made me a cup of tea. I apologised for the upset, she consoled me saying, "You did the right thing, no one could live like that." Actually I don't think Mary had ever really liked him, she guessed he was arrogant.

I stayed that night with Mary and Dave. Next day I registered at the labour exchange for employment, and purchased the evening paper to look for a bedsit.

I had to keep going now I dared not let myself sit down and think. I must admit I did think John would try to contact me, but he never did.

Within two days I had secured a job in a nearby village pub, housekeeping for a brother and sister, live in and £15 a week. It was a very picturesque little place with a nice big park and a few shops scattered around.

❋

I was still devastated and registered with a nearby doctor for moral support. I was also scared of the depression returning. I usually had a delayed reaction, which was more severe. Again I was lucky with my doctor, who spent some time talking things through with me and put me on anti depressants.

I threw myself into my job and prayed, my family rallied around, encouraging me. I clenched my teeth and kept on working, determined to remain as independent as I could. Strangely enough I never shed a tear. I did feel very stupid to have made such a big mistake for the second time in my life and to have lost my home that was so hard in the first place to put around me.

Once more it was sink or swim and it was the depression I found the hardest to cope with; it's something you cannot communicate to another human being. On my days off I walked around the park, often wishing I could just keep walking. Those were very dark days.

My doctor kept reminding me to remember the song *One day at a Time Sweet Jesus*. Yes indeed, there is an awful lot in that song. I also felt I had left my children down so badly in marrying again, I was full of guilt.

I had to reapply to the council for a house and I was bottom of the list. I also made an application to a housing association, a group that had not long started up to house people in difficult circumstances. I also contacted a solicitor but as the marriage was of short duration I was doubtful I would get anything.

After a court hearing, an unpleasant experience again, because of my age and circumstances I did get £10 maintenance a week to be paid through the courts. With the reaction to all that had happened I was unable to cope with the job and 7 months had passed.

I got a bedsit in Warwick that needed decorating. I signed on for unemployment benefit. I was near the family and usually had dinner with them in turn on Sundays and I was involved with the grandchildren.

❋

By this time I had 6 of them. Annie's was the youngest. I took him for walks in his pram filling the days best I could.

I was decorating the bedsit and stood on a chair one day to change bulbs when I fell and broke my wrist. I remember it was a very wet day. I walked to the hospital and it was put in plaster. Then I couldn't do much for 6 weeks.

I was living near my friend Sarah Campbell again and she was very kind to me. When I visited her she always served me nice tea and cake nicely presented on a tray, being a counsellor she was very understanding.

After 12 months I had a letter from my solicitor saying John had conveniently made himself redundant from his job, in which case he could not be forced to continue the maintenance of £10 a week. Although it was a loss to me I was in a way relieved as I felt now that really severed the relationship completely and in 2 more years I could automatically divorce him.

I went back to see my Priest, explaining all that had happened, as of course up to now I could not receive the sacraments. He in turn explained to me as a Catholic the registry office marriage was not recognised by the church, though it was of course legally binding, so I could now go to confession as long as there were no other ties. I was now free to go to the sacraments. He wished me well and hoped that my health would now improve and I could be happy.

The lease was up on the house I had the bedsit in so I was house hunting again. After a few weeks I got a small flat at the back of a large house.

Financially the family were helping me out as much as they could. I really was not up to holding a job down. I hated the flat, it had a long dark hall.

These again were lonely days, the only consolation was that I was on my own and not upsetting any one else and feeling very much my situation was self inflicted. Strangely enough I didn't blame John and I wasn't bitter towards him, it was just a very hard lesson to learn.

I was still being treated for clinical depression. An Irish girl occupied the flat in the front of the house and we became friends. She made nice porter cake and often invited me around for tea. She had a very dry sense of humour and told me when she first saw me walking through the hall with my bags she thought, "Lord, this one looks very posh." She thought it was hilarious that I risked marriage again, especially to a man of a different culture. She was very wary of men since looking after several brothers in Mayo before emigrating to England.

I wasn't writing home much any more since the death of my mother, and father being blind he couldn't read letters. I 'phoned him from time to time but never mentioned the marriage to him as he would have thought I had taken leave of my senses, so he never knew. I did keep in touch with Noeleen back home, and of course my old pal Mary, also Mai and Tommy Foley, they did support me as much as they could. We weren't a close family ourselves as my sisters split up very young when emigrating to England and the U.S.A. Lena in Bedfordshire kept in touch, and my sister in the States.

Time rolled on and I was told Andy was very amused at the breakdown of the marriage. He was at this time himself involved with a Scots woman. As Billy was away and still unattached and planning on returning to Warwickshire I was hoping to get a two bedroom house at least.

I had a goal another challenge awaiting me. The housing association offices were 4 flights up a building, no lifts. I lost count of the times I walked up those stairs. The staff were lovely people and so helpful. They were aware of exactly how I lost my council house and were easy to talk to. The committee consisted of doctors, solicitors, a Priest and I had a doctor recommending me because of the background of depression. I did have great hopes of a two bedroom house having some work done on it. So this kept me going.

❋

On completion in 1981 it was decided to give me the house. It was £12 a week. It had a small front garden and a long narrow back garden. I was delighted to move into my own house again. Annie bought my three piece suite, Mary and Dave carpeted the house, Mags bought my bed, Joseph gave me cash to get wardrobes, and it had central heating.

Billy came back to live with me and tiled the bathroom and kitchen and built a small porch on the front, he also put a shed in the back garden and got himself a little dog named Sailor. He started work in a car factory. The family always helped me out, they were very generous.

A new house, good neighbours, and a nice area - it gave me a lift, and I felt better in myself. I helped the family out with the grandchildren, and with Billy to take care of I was busy. I liked gardening and soon got an apple tree in. Billy put some paving slabs down. I had garden pots scattered around with colourful blooms in spring. Billy built a wooden shed for his ferrets. He liked hunting in the country with his dog.

I soon got to know a lot of people in the street, meeting them at mass, mostly Irish. One lady, named Ellen, was a nurse in the local hospital and soon we became friends and we would visit each other.

I made a pilgrimage to Lourdes, which was a lovely experience, and got the opportunity to reflect back on my life.

It was the end of November, I was 64 and busy making the family cakes and puddings which was the usual thing at Christmas time. Billy was sitting in the living room playing with our cat. I just checked the cake in the oven and was preparing the evening meal and feeling a bit tired. I thought, 'I'm glad it's a stew today, just a one pot meal,' when I got severe chest pain.

❋

Billy called the ambulance - it was a heart attack. I was in hospital very quickly and detained for 3 weeks and made a slow recovery but it was 12 months before I felt reasonably well and able to cope with my affairs. Then it was good to go for a walk again and I viewed the world differently. I still had angina, and depression hovered all the time. I handled it by thinking, 'Tomorrow will be better,' and I was never short of brainwaves. I always tried to have a goal whatever that may-be, changing the furniture around or decorating a room, but eventually I got a great longing to return home to Ireland.

I always bought *Irelands Own* magazine, it kept me in touch. I would occasionally see houses for exchange between England and Ireland. First I wrote to the corporation back home consulting with the housing association. The replies were favourable; there would be no objection to such a trans-action as long as both rents were clear of arrears, but they did tell me in Ireland they had never actually had it happen. I did advertise in *Ireland Own* and *Irish Post*. I had one reply, but it was a rough area in Dublin so I declined.

My family were all living about 4 or 5 miles in distance from me. My youngest grandchild now 13, it seemed my work was now completed. I had lots of cousins and friends back home. I was now 66.

Imagining all the family coming to visit in turn. Where we had lived at home was so well placed 7 or 8 miles from some beautiful seaside resorts and Ireland was very close to my heart.

My friend Mary and her husband had also gone back to live there and my family thought it was a good idea but as yet only pie in the sky. I was in my back garden working one afternoon when Billy came through the back gate. He had just heard from someone that if we surrendered our house now the H.A would give us x amount of money; this gave me food for thought.

The following morning I 'phoned the repair department as I had a leak from a pipe in my bathroom. I then asked to be put through to management with an inquiry about the incentive scheme asking, if it was in operation. I was told, "Yes indeed it is, but we only have one offer left. I would have to send you out a form straight away."

The offer was made - that was 1990. But he did try to discourage me. The agent knew we were good tenants and had improved the house a great deal; he also knew I had been ill. He told me that what I could buy in Ireland would possibly be very run down.

I discussed this with Billy, who was very anxious to live in Ireland. He had £6000 saved. I got in touch with my friend Noeleen; she thought it was a great idea and suggested staying with her, giving me a chance to look around.

I did make the trip home and after much searching found a small house selling at £14,000 and needing a lot of repairs but it had potential and was very central. It had been let out to students for a few years and had to be absolutely cleared and decorated throughout.

After 3 weeks I returned to England and the hassle was only beginning. We were communicating with the auctioneers and solicitors in Ireland plus paper work with the housing association. The punt and sterling exchange was good, a big move, but I prayed to God, 'Don't let me make a mistake, it is my last chance'.

There was all the packing and arranging transport, for the move. I took all the furniture with me. I can't say I was unhappy leaving England, yet I did feel sad as the children had grown up there, and it had given me a fresh start in life, but it had never been my choice to leave Ireland so closing the door and saying goodbye to neighbours family and friends was a wrench of course. I knew the family would visit me and I would visit them so this was yet another beginning.

❋

The house we purchased in Ireland had no central heating and needed a lot of work done. The first thing I did was light a coal fire, it was long time since I had seen a coal fire. With the arrival of the furniture, relatives helped Billy and myself unload. We got rid of all the rubbish and pulled up old carpets.

The bathroom was very basic with walls half tiled, the bath which was old. There was a small back yard and nice sized garden to the back and large coal bunkers. It had a pretty hallway and staircase which led to two attic bedrooms. Some windows needed replacing, also the back kitchen roof. Billy would eventually deal with all the repair work but he kept strictly to that. All the other work like cosmetic work, papering and painting, was my problem.

The fireplace which had a tiled surround was in very bad condition and the grate was burned out and had to be replaced, so I decided to give the old tiles a few coats of cream emulsion. When completed it looked good, the disadvantage was I had to touch up the tiles every six weeks to keep it looking good. The broken tiles in front of the grate were replaced and I gave them a few coats of paint.

I bought some cheap hard wearing carpet for the hall. Before leaving England I had purchased some good quality cream carpet from the auction rooms cheap to cover the stairs. I covered the kitchen floor with lino also the bathroom, and painted the shabby old wall tiles. Billy attached a hand shower to the tap fixed to the wall that we used to have a quick shower.

I picked up some cheap, mostly chipboard paper, for the walls with white emulsion. Windows were washed down nets and curtains put up, it now looked fresh and clean. Billy's cousin helped with the ceilings and paint work and Billy and himself collected a lot of old quarry multi colour stones, making the back garden quite attractive. The old kitchen sink and toilet were arranged to hold plants and together with my pot plants transformed the garden.

✼

The wiring was in poor shape but my cousin was an electrician and made all that safe. We got our side lamps up for Christmas, a nice fire going, and our house looked very cosy.

I was only a short while home when I was offered a job; 3 days a week in a little shop 3 doors away from me, which was a great help financially. I was 67. The extra money allowed me to borrow and get double glazed windows. We had a little house warming party to thank everyone that helped. Everyone enjoyed the night and the house was very much admired.

The phone was already installed in the house it just needed reconnecting. It was a miracle, everything fell into place and within 6 months we were settled. My Irish pension was sorted out I just had enough stamps to qualify for the entitlements. In the meantime Billy had returned to England to work and the following summer he came home to finish off the work left undone, like roofing and converting part of the living room. It had originally been a dining room but wasn't used as the kitchen was quite spacious. We now had a three bed-roomed house.

It was lovely to walk around the city again remembering school days all the old familiar streets, especially our own home and my grandmother's, and the ballroom where I had enjoyed so many dances now long ago. It was a bit of a culture shock to begin with having spent 48 years in England, where everything was so impersonal and one didn't make friends easily, except the people you met at work or mass and your immediate neighbours, but you still didn't belong.

I was in touch with the family, all anxious to know how I was settling in and they 'phoned and wrote often. It was great to have my bus pass, giving me the opportunity to visit the seaside where I had taken the children so often in the summertime in the 1950's. I had cousins living there that I had helped to raise as a young teenager.

My youngest daughter came on holidays also Joseph and his wife Mary. Something was happening all the time keeping me busy. The friendship with my old friend Noeleen petered out I was so busy getting my life together decorating. The money was very tight and I was under a lot of pressure. Noeleen felt I came home to retire and that I should have more time to spend relaxing, that's okay in theory but put into practice it doesn't always work out.

I had one or two set backs with the angina, but nothing too serious.

I registered with my doctor who remembered my mother and father as his patients.

I had several relatives scattered around the city. James and his wife Jane, though much younger than me, made me so welcome, offering to help where they could. Jane was my counsellor, we laugh about that now, I 'phoned her if I had a problem or needed advice.

Paul offered to read over my book as I attempted to write my story I valued his opinion. His wife Clair did the typing for me. John and Pat were the organisers and most obliging. Pat is quite unique in disposition and very caring and sincere and she was my financial adviser. They had two children, Aine and Desmond. I entertained Aine with my stories of long ago. The key was always in the door for me.

I was about 3 years back in Ireland and visiting Pat and John at their home by the seaside. On one of my many invitations to dinner we were discussing a cottage that was for sale not too far from where they lived. Again it needed a lot doing to it. Ideally I would have chosen to live by the sea, imagining myself walking the beach in my retirement and the family visiting in the summer.

At the time I was having a problem heating my house, except for the fire in the living room I only had an oil heater in the kitchen and an electric wall heater in the bathroom. We had improved the house so much I thought it was worth while having it valued, the cost to have put central heating in was so expensive.

❋

It was Christmas time. I got all my decorations up, nice fire blazing away and I was making my puddings and cake when the estate agent phoned saying the house had doubled in value and had someone to view it that day. There was a lot of interest. I believe presentation is important, and with the atmosphere of Christmas that was to my advantage. Billy and myself were surprised we had managed to achieve so much with little money in such a short time.

We got an offer for our house, so enabling us to purchase the cottage at the seaside, this also was very run down. But with very careful managing the profit we made went on repairs. It was a lovely cosy cottage 10 minutes walk from the sea. Our front garden was a sun trap and standing on the front steps of the house I could get a glimpse of the sea. A thick hedge surrounded the house where the birds were nesting and we could hear the sounds of the sea at night - a little bit of heaven really. I celebrated my 70th birthday by the seaside and my cousins had a lovely party for me..

Before I tackled the decorating of the house I walked the beach and gazed around the promenade, where all the old amusements used to be that my children enjoyed in the early

50's, remembering the places we sat on the beach; I could almost see them race to the sea.

Annie being the youngest was scared of the water, so I held her hands as she paddled, then when the tide came too close for comfort we gathered our wet togs and towels along with the bag packed with sandwiches and scones or maybe apple tarts, and made for the fields leading off the prom, where I spread out an old table cloth for our meal.

Joseph took the big enamel teapot to one of the nearby cottages that supplied boiling water for 2p and we enjoyed our meal. The sand always managed to get into the sandwiches, but these were washed down with the hot tea that always tasted so good by the seaside. Eventually we gathered our belongings and made our way, tired and often sunburned, to the train for home.

I then recalled the lovely old dance hall now long gone and replaced by amusement arcades and ice cream parlours. The gypsy caravans also coming to mind, so loudly and elaborately decorated, where the gypsy herself stood at the door, luring you to enter her lucky caravan. "I can tell you so much dearie, don't pass the gypsy. Just cross my hand with silver." Resisting because you didn't have the money, and consoling yourself it was a sin anyway, and how could you face the Priest and tell him you had your fortune told by a gypsy?

Imagine the penance you would get. So that helped a lot to console yourself.

As the memories flooded into my mind I climbed the hill back to my newly purchased cottage. A big challenge again awaiting me, still it kept me going, once again papering and painting, Billy tiled the bathroom and turned the small back bedroom into a kitchen which he fitted and tiled. I painted my little hall red with all white doors. In a few months it was comfortable.

Billy returned to England to work. I started on my front garden and got help to slab the front making an attractive patio. Soon I had pots scattered about for my bulbs and plants. I was surprised to have achieved so much once more in just 4 years and my favourite hymn came to mind, *How Great Thou Art*' especially as I walked the beach in the summer evenings and saw such beautiful sunsets. From my bedroom I could see the sun rise in the morning over the sea, making you feel it was good to be alive.

The family took their turn to visit me in the summertime. Mary and husband Dave came in the summer of 1997 and she loved the house. She was very artistic and put her own little touch to everything before leaving.

THE DEATH OF MARY

It was mid August 1999 that the devastating news came - my beautiful daughter Mary had been diagnosed with ovarian cancer. Every fibre of my being was crying out, 'No, this cannot be true. Please God it will go away.' With chemo she went into remission for 2 years. Instinctively I knew I was going to lose her. I prayed and prayed, but back it came. Still, I hoped for a miracle.

When we spoke on the phone she was cheerful and positive, assuring me she felt fine and would be having more chemo. She was doing her best to calm my fears and discourage me from going over to England, telling me there was nothing I could do and advising me to enjoy the summer by the sea, and then go over to her for Christmas.

This was August 2001 and I left for England a few weeks later. It was a sad journey. Mary was 53 years old and had one son. She worked as a carer for 11 years in an old people's home. Mary was a very private girl and did not socialise much but had a lovely home which she was devoted to. She was so full of love and was always happy with a great sense of humour. I only remember her to have 2 holidays in her lifetime.

I am finding it quite difficult to write about this part of my life, we are a very close family especially emotionally, and the grief we feel is indescribable. Mary herself was very positive but this would be typical of my darling, always considering every one else. This tragedy had come up so unexpectedly in our lives and those were very sad and strange days - like you are on the edge of a volcano.

It was Tuesday November 13th 2001 and the Macmillan nurse was visiting Mary to discuss home nursing, which we

BRIGID PATRICIA BOGGAN

all as a family wished to be involved in as she wanted to die at home.

❄

We all had the opportunity to talk with Mary in great depth, it was painful and sad and her courage to say the least was remarkable. We had been told by the specialist at the hospital that it was only a matter of weeks. Possibly she may see Christmas, but by which time they would expect her to be very unwell.

It was all so unreal. I tried to pray and told myself, 'It happens to everyone in time.' But it's no consolation, nothing makes sense and you just get through the days mechanically. I was staying with my son Joseph and family, sitting by the fire, it was a very cold day and I was waiting for the 'phone to ring with information about what the nurse had to say about the home care.

Mary phoned me the night before, to say she had been to Leamington with her son and had a perfectly wonderful day. They visited Rachams and purchased his Christmas gifts and then had lunch together. She said he was so brave and just said, "Well mum, it's going to happen to us all one day." Then she told me she loved me and said good night and promised to ring me the next day, so I was waiting.

24th November. 11 days on and Mary was still coping and refused to give in. I baked some vanilla slices for her

180

that morning but when I called she was up and dressed to go to town with Mags, just for an hour as she tired easily. Her cousin Bernie slept with her some nights as she needed some space from us, Bernie is very kind.

Mary also got the idea into her head that she may die in her sleep. Her son Jack seemed to be accepting it but it was very hard to judge him. Her husband Dave was devastated. Mary was determined she would not have the GP or nurse until the end and absolutely necessary. She was keeping us together and reminding us that she got 53 years after all, and we will all walk the same path and she won't be here to help us.

Mary spent her whole life reaching out and helping others she was unique and I'm proud to be her mother.

※

Mary struggled on and kept on her feet up to Christmas, and went shopping with Mags for the Christmas gifts which she distributed to all of us the week before Christmas. She then developed bad headaches and a scan revealed small tumours in several areas of the brain. It was downhill all the way from then on, but she was still on her feet, but struggling.

She had a driver or pump around her waist with the syringe inserted to get the pain killer into her system. Christmas Eve she was very ill and was in bed for the first time Christmas day, but still determined to walk to the bathroom. By this time I was sleeping with her. Annie and Mags were taking turns to sleep on a mattress by the bed, as Mary got very restless at night.

Early January it was no longer possible to continue the home nursing. It was painful for her to get out of bed, the Macmillan nurse talked her into going into the hospice where she could have specialist care and be stabilized on drugs to make her more comfortable. The hospice was marvellous, though very ill she joked with nurses and co-operated with everyone. She was so vulnerable and heart breaking to watch. I stayed all night with her on the Tuesday but she was unconscious. She was anointed at 2 a.m. on Ash Wednesday 13th February 2002, and she died that night at 10.45p.m.

Annie sang her favourite hymns to her and as she sang *Sweet Sacrament Most Holy,* Mary took her last breath and left us all. We were gathered around her, Mags, Annie and myself. As I said my goodbye to Mary I couldn't help but think, "It's all over for you now sweetheart, you only have to do it once. You've landed now and you're there where nothing will ever hurt you again." I can recall two things she said before she became unconscious, "I wish it was all over," and once she called out, "Oh God, help me."

THE SEASIDE AUGUST 2002

It was now almost 6 months since my darling Mary's death and life was not the same. But people were very good, and I had counselling from a very kind and compassionate lady; she cried with me during our talks. I found it a great consolation to discuss everything with someone outside the family, where I could be myself and not just pretend I was fine. As a family we were protecting each other rather than consoling one another.

Those days I cried a lot, I felt her very close sometimes. I still remember all the things she said to me like, "Mum, I will leave such strength behind me you will cope with this." This still spurs me on, and the conviction that she is in Heaven and at peace in her heavenly home. While I am still on my physical journey, I know that for sure one day I will see her again.

The stages of grief are each so hard. First the disbelief, like you are just acting out a scene or it's a bad dream you will wake up from. Then the normality of the world around you, when nothing is normal to you. Going over and over it all again in the time we had together and we laughed and cried and talked almost about everything. She was so brave but she did think she would slip away in her sleep.

Unfortunately she still had mountains to climb without knowing it, and still she never complained. But it was so hard to watch to the bitter end. She did call on her God and I know he was listening. Her wish was to be cremated and her ashes to be buried with me in Ireland.

August 10th 2002. It's Saturday morning and the sun is shining. I can glimpse the sea from my door I have the wind chimes Mary gave me hanging in the porch; little pink and blue birds, making lovely sounds in the gentle breeze. A white butterfly is moving to and fro, and I think, 'Maybe that's you darling, sending me a message of comfort.'

❋

It's been a tearful morning. I was taking cuttings from a beautiful plant Mary had given me when I became very sad. She had a great way with plants and she loved everything that grew in her garden. She was so artistic and had a gift of putting everything into perspective, so very talented.

To lose your child is like losing part of yourself and there are no shortcuts through the grief; it comes in waves and then the flashbacks of her dying. I think of Our Lady of Sorrows - she watched her son die on the cross so why not me? I can honestly say for months before she died, Mary was always considering us, sparing our feelings all the time.

I am sure lots of people reading this can identify with me, but even that's no consolation. A lady put her hand on my arm one day in the church and said, "My dear these are the crosses that are getting us to heaven, and the way to Jesus for some is very hard, and our minds are not big enough to contain the reason for suffering."

I'm so lucky with my doctor and all staff at the surgery, including our Priest and nuns at the convent, friends like Lucy on the Old Road, Annie and Joan, Joe and Margaret.

The white butterfly has passed the window again, I'm sure it's the same one. It's particularly peaceful here this morning. I can almost hear Mary's laughter. She was always laughing and had a great sense of humour, and she was beautiful to look at and always giving.

From the age of 11 she was eager to help out in the house, and was the little mother floating about the place. When I had the nervous breakdown and hospitalized for 9 weeks, I think back now wondering how they managed when I was almost oblivious to everything about me. Guilt creeps into grief, and I think, 'If only all that had not happened, I'm sure her life would have been a lot happier.'

I thanked her before she died; it was the day before she became unconscious and she said, "Please, no mum." Thanks seemed so little to say to my angel.

❋

This part of the book is so difficult to pen. When I started this book I never imagined I would lose Mary or think I had yet another hurdle to jump. While she was very sick, in her last days and I climbed into bed and I would cry out to Jesus, "How will I watch her suffer?" I felt he was holding out his hands to me as if to say, "I am here, you can do it. I'll never leave you." I get great comfort from the charismatic prayer groups, the coming together of people who are so warm and caring as they reach out.

August 16th 2002. It's another glorious day praise God, and I am tidying up my front garden. I am peaceful today and just enjoying the sun. My cat Queenie is romping around and chasing anything that moves. I have the radio close by, the songs are very nostalgic, and the little white butterfly is drifting to and fro and I keep wondering if it's the same one.

I started remembering when I first came to this pretty resort and the pleasure it gave me; getting into my runners and track suit and walking the beach in my early 70's listening to the gentle sound of the waves. I was appreciating everything so much more now, even the smell of the seaweed in September. You could actually smell the iodine as you approached the sea and it was known to be very healthy indeed to bathe at this particular time of year, especially if you suffered with arthritis.

I enjoyed the beautiful sunsets - things I never noticed before. Youth is really wasted on the young. When I took my children for day trips on the train to the amusement park, where music was played and the hobby horses attracted them; going round and round in the chair planes that swung high into the air, the bumper cars were another attraction, all long gone now and replaced with much more elaborate equipment. Cars now lined the promenade, replacing the horse and cart.

❉

And in the background an old gramophone played *Oh Play To Me Gypsy* and *Just Cross My Palm With Silver*, and you were wishing you had a shilling, wondering what she could see in the crystal ball, but then you would have to go to confession as you had broken the first commandment so you just shrugged and sighed and felt glad you had resisted the temptation.

As I looked up from the beach I was reminded of the grand old dance hall where all the great band sounds played the music that never really died away, *Auf Wiederzehen, It's Almost Tomorrrow, Mr. Wonderful.* I could go on and on about the bittersweet era of the 40's. I continued my walk down the sandy and pebbled beach that took you towards the sand hills. The late summer and early winter walks meant fewer people on the beach, except the residents exercising their dogs.

Making sure there was no one in ear shot I sang *I Watch the Sunrise* and said a decade of the rosary, in thanksgiving for getting me through all the bad times with the strength and incentive to carry on. Climbing back up the hill to the villa which led to my home, leaning over the wall I had a great view of the beach.

My thoughts again went back to when the children were small and we sat together making sand castles and waited for the tide to come in, when there would be a race for the sea. Annie was just walking, she wasn't very keen on the water and I stood holding her hand as she paddled with Billy, not missing the opportunity to splash her.

The sea air gave us all a great appetite, it was not unusual to hear the children say, "Mammy I'm starving," as I shared out the food and cups of tea in even amounts. There would be remarks like, "She or he got more than me!" Still we all ate heartily before gathering the wet towels and togs and making our way back to the train, with lots of sand in our shoes, and sunburned arms and legs.

✳

All seemed so long ago now, yet still vivid in my memory. It was usually baking soda, or if you had it, sour milk, that you applied to the sunburn, assuring the children it would be a lot better in the morning, and they might wake up with a nice tan. But it was far more likely the skin would peel and flake off leaving ugly red patches that got itchy. Camomile lotion helped to soothe this.

LEAVING THE SEASIDE TOWN MARCH 2003

Another year has passed. 13th February 03 was a hard day. I cried a lot at Mary's mass. It was so unreal hearing her name read from the altar. But you just go through the motions of the day, knowing there is nothing else you can do.

I gave a lot of thought as to how I could change the last years of my life, surely I could do something. I was very cut off in my little house although it was comfortable and near the beach. I wasn't as well as I was last year; Mary's death had left a big void in my life.

The garden was getting too much for me to look after. One of the nuns from the convent called regularly and we had lovely chats. Anne continued to counsel me and my cousins were always available on the 'phone if I needed someone to talk to. Still the empty feeling never left me.

On wakening one morning I decided the time had come for yet another decision in my life, perhaps there was something I could do after all. The house was co-owned with Billy. He had worked very hard on both houses and had transformed them. On my death the house would go to him.

However life has many twists to it, and my circumstances had changed dramatically, so I decided to approach Billy and suggest selling the house. This was eventually agreed to, so I had the house valued and surprisingly it sold within 4 weeks.

❄

I had already applied for an apartment back in town; these were for retired people and it was a good situation, near shops and the church. I was interviewed and successful in getting one of these, a one bedroom with a nice view. With a down payment and moderate rent, as I had some money now to come from the house, this wasn't a problem. And I knew several of the residents since my younger days.

Preparing the house for sale, packing, making yet another big move was very distressing, leaving behind cousins and such good friends I made at the seaside, but at least I had realised my dream. I had a good 8 years by the sea, enjoyed my little house and garden, had lovely walks on the beach, had seen the rough and calm seas and found time to gather my thoughts.

This time however I had some finances. God does work in mysterious ways indeed. My daughter Mags came home from England to help me move without her help I couldn't have got through it all. It was so hard to deal with mentally and physically and I really wasn't up to it. Mags stayed with me a month until it was all over and I was settled once more back in town in my apartment. It was a wrench leaving the seaside but I am still in easy reach by bus to the beach.

I was christened in the cathedral close by 78 years ago, and now after all the moving and travelling I am back in the same parish, having done the full circle. The house I was born in is still standing and as I pass it I always touch the door. I have some lovely memories of this city: the bridge itself that I took my first step to reach the factory I worked in at fifteen, and the big step when I left my beloved city on the train that took us to England, where we lived and survived for 48 years.

14th AUGUST 2003

I am settled in my apartment almost 5 months, relaxed and happy it's very cosy. I love to hear the bells ring out on Sunday mornings from the church. Our gardens in front are beautifully kept and well shaded by the mature trees.

Having now met all the residents, some younger and some older than myself, we relate well to each other. The conservatory is a pleasant setting where coffee mornings are held and we can meet for a chat. There is also a comfortable lounge area and seats are arranged outside if we wish to sit in the sun. All the amenities are close by. I am fortunate indeed. In addition I am enjoying the beautiful hot weather, and having free transport making it easy for me to visit the seaside. I still enjoy my walks on the beach. I get the 8:30 a.m. bus out and come back on the 12:45 p.m. enjoying the lovely views of the countryside.

This morning I had a late breakfast in O'Neills Hotel close to the beach, very enjoyable it has a nice atmosphere. I am pinching myself, I really can't believe I have all this time on my hands, no more rushing around with family to look after. But a void will always be there as I no longer have my lovely daughter Mary. Her birthday is next month and she would love this weather. Her garden was so beautifully arranged she loved forget-me-nots. No doubt she is enjoying eternal sunshine, strolling amidst the unimaginable flowers, with her little brother by the hand.

BRIGID PATRICIA BOGGAN

Our beautiful weather continues and it's so uplifting. It is evening time, just getting dark and I'm playing a relaxing disc, *Red Roses for a Blue Lady*. I'm sentimental as ever, I can still lose myself in music.

Reaching this stage of my life my bad experiences have taught me a lot. I hope I am more tolerant and have learned something from everything that has ever happened to me.

Possibly all the storms of life you pass through happen so the better you can be born. Perhaps the situation you find yourself in is the way your life was meant to be. It is within your ability to cope with almost everything, the key lies in trusting, and having patience, reminding yourself it can't always be raining.

Forgiving someone who really hurt you is very hard but it is possible to forgive. You make a decision. Forgetting is the problem because you have a mind and the bruise hangs on in there that does not go. Still you can try looking out more and not in like we do because we are human. We are after all just human beings, emotionally imperfect and striving for peace and happiness.

We could go on questioning everything that happens to us, getting us nowhere. Our minds are not big enough to contain or understand the ways of God. I try to think I am unique and that he made me the way I am; he sees into my heart and loves me just as I am with all my imperfections. I find that a great comfort. I also believe trouble is very evenly distributed. A saying that I believe rings true is, "If in life everyone put their troubles in a heap on the floor, you would walk away with your own." My youngest son once said to me, "Go to any window in the world and look in. You will find the same problems there except in a different form. This gave me food for thought.

SEPTEMBER 1st 2003

A beautiful sunny morning and I got the 10 a.m. bus to the seaside. As I walked along the promenade and then on the beach it was warm with still some holiday makers about. The tide was in and the sun glistened and shimmered on the water. A fleet of tiny birds were swarming down as they do, in the shape of a plane, landing for a few seconds at the edge of the water as it gently ebbed in on the beach.

It was amazing to watch the flow of the sea, something that can be so destroying can also be so soothing and calm. I heard people talking about the dolphins that were seen further down the beach that morning, though I did not actually see them myself.

The sky was so blue, with grey to white clouds in wide thick sweeps here and there and the sky seemed to envelop the beach itself. The spire of the church appeared as the centre piece of the town. You could feel the spirituality of the place. The hymn, *How Great Thou Art* crossed my mind once more.

As a small sailing boat drifted gently on the calm water I took my shoes off and walked along the edge of the water and could smell the seaweed. I felt so privileged to experience such peace in my day.

September continued to be a lovely warm end to our summer. Towards the end of the month I did not feel good in myself, my back and legs ached a lot and I slowed up in my walking. Almost overnight I was hit with sciatica down my left side and leg - it was very disabling. My doctor started me on painkillers, which I had a bad reaction to, causing me to have stomach problem.

Early one morning, mid October I had an angina attack. Pushing the panic button to alert the caretaker, the ambulance was called for. I was in hospital for 9 days, where I had x-rays scans angiogram given lots of antibiotics for my stomach problems. The nursing was good and the doctors were excellent. My daughter Annie came home from England and took me back with her for Christmas where I stayed with Mags and her husband for 6 weeks.

The sciatica still lingered on and I was using a stick to take the pressure off the leg, overnight life had changed, and I lacked energy.

❈

All my family were in England; 2 daughters, 1 son, 3 grand daughters and 5 great grandchildren, so I had lots of company My daughter-in-law and the three grandchildren, my family were all within easy reach of each other.

Out of the blue a nice one bedroom bungalow became available to rent, again within easy reach of all the family. I returned to Ireland and my apartment with Mags and we discussed yet another move for me. Looking at my situation from all angles it was the most sensible thing to do. I was beginning to feel very unsure of myself now and the family were concerned for me living alone. My cousins also agreed it was in my own interest to go back to England and the security of my family.

I have arranged to take all my furniture back with me to England. My family are busy in my little bungalow, painting and having carpets laid; they are so good preparing for my return. My cousins here are arranging to have a party for me and doing all they can to help and my friends are calling round. My special nun was with me today and we had a great chat and promised to keep in touch. My friends Anne and Lucy are arranging to meet me next week. I am so lucky with people I met.

I will visit the seaside next week to say goodbye to the charismatic prayer group. I will always remember my cousins that did so much to help me and all the wonderful friends I came in contact with in my 13 years in Ireland. The city itself holds bittersweet memories for me. I will miss so many things and yet it is another new beginning; I am rejoining my family that has increased so much in 13 years.

My farewell party went off very well at my cousins by the seaside, so carefully arranged for me. They presented me with beautiful Waterford crystal; I was very touched to know they cared so much. During my stay in hospital they visited me daily, taking my washing and returning it nicely laundered and making sure I had everything I needed. That kind of dedication can never be repaid, it's unconditional.

Despite all my troubles I was very lucky to have such good relatives and friends to support me.

final chapter

JANUARY 2004

THE REALIZATION NOW WAS SETTING IN, the step I was about to take was indeed a very daunting one. It all seemed too much to take in as I was still struggling with the sciatica and using a stick, my mobility wasn't good. Depression was never far away. This was as bad as the pain and somehow I couldn't talk about it, I just kept telling myself, "You can't let it get to you now, you're too busy to get sick."

Notice had to be given to the administrator of the apartments to terminate the agreement for health reasons, notify the pensions department and all the little things to attend to like electricity 'phone bills etc. Removal firm were engaged as I couldn't pack anything this time. My family kept in touch from England about the details of the rent and so many other things.

But one night it just got too much and I thought, 'I just can't go through with it; I can't make the journey.' Mags had returned to England after a week to pursue the bungalow and help to get it organised for me. She looked tired and had her own life and responsibilities, and I felt guilty about putting too much responsibility on to her.

I had a district nurse calling and home help would be arranged and I was having physiotherapy, still the future was uncertain. My daughter wouldn't be able to keep travelling backwards and forwards when I was ill. And it was a big responsibility for my cousins keeping my family informed, so there seemed no doubt about the fact I had no choice.

❉

I intend to be buried in Ireland and have Mary's ashes buried with me. I attended to all these details so that when the time came all this would be taken care of. I guess it's when you are weakest its, then you are strong.

Tomorrow is 13th February and Mary's 2nd anniversary. I still can't grasp it's been 2 years, and life still goes on. The quotation comes to mind, "We can die or make a harvest of our wounds." I will attend her anniversary mass in the morning and once again go through the day as normally as possible.

I saw everything through the removals, all packed and labelled, all my furniture ready for transport to England.

On February 23rd my cousins drove me to the airport. It was hard leaving Ireland after 13 years. We said our goodbyes. At this stage I didn't feel much emotion and everything was so mechanical. My daughter Mags was at the airport to meet me. I stayed with her until March 2nd and then moved into my bungalow.

My furniture had arrived from Ireland on February 28th unpacked and put it in place. All I did was help to unpack my clothes. Mags, Annie and cousin Bernie had done all the decorating and laying out of the furniture. My son-in-law Bill had also done a lot of decorating for me. The bungalow was really beautiful and well situated, with just 13 houses for retired couples, some living alone. It had one bedroom and the living room looked onto a very mature, interesting garden, with a large fenced in paddock behind it with horses trotting around and beautiful chestnut trees that appeared to touch the sky. The garden has a lovely lawn with two small patios. It's a dream. There is an open plan front and a nice lawn and the landlord has a maintenance man that cuts the lawns, so I will only have potting plants to attend to, if I wish.

Nice size kitchen, bathroom and hallway. I just walked around admiring it for hours. All my furniture fitted in so well. It is all double glazed and efficiently heated.

❋

Still a bit slow walking but so glad the pain has eased. I do have some numbness in my foot I am not really expecting it to go altogether.

I am now 79 and still getting about, thankfully. I would hope to continue to be as independent as I could. I do have a dread of being a burden. I am dealing with once again attending to all the filling in of forms for change of pension, phone connections, electricity and new doctor, which I find pretty stressful, still it keeps me alert.

Annie takes me shopping to a big store for my groceries and drives me back home and puts my shopping away. I think she finds my slow walking irritating. Mags walks quite a lot with me still I do hold her back I was always so quick doing everything I am very aware when anyone walks with me I am holding them back.

April 18th I am now 6 weeks in my new house in England. Some of my neighbours have knocked on my door to welcome me. One man rolls my dustbins out for me, so kind, and offering to do any heavy lifting for me. My son-in-law Bill is still coming to do odd jobs for me. My son Billy 'phoned me from Ireland today. He was in good form and glad I'm settling once again. Joseph is not a good visitor but he and his wife have called twice and are giving me space to settle in.

Today I did some gardening, there's a lot of tidying up to do. It's a haven for birds so I put my bird cage out filled with peanuts in the paddock behind my garden. I have two huge chestnut trees coming into bloom. Annie gave me a beautiful oak garden seat she had made in memory of Mary with a brass plate engraved, 'Forever sisters Mary, Mags and Annie.'

I sit on it remembering and wishing she was sitting with me too, enjoying the lovely scenery and listening to the birds, and when I cry I recall her saying, "Of course you will cry mum." She was so wise.

The regret I have is that I never told her how much I really loved and appreciated her, because deep down I always knew she was very special and unique, yet I never told her. Yes, I have remorse about that, she never knew she was very special to me and she gave so much of herself and was so unassuming.

I didn't get around to visiting my new great grand children yet, I am not close to any church here but Mags takes me to mass on Saturday night or Sunday morning. The school is still there where my children went to and where I took them to mass when they were small.

THE INTEGRITY OF SOLITUDE

I think solitude is good, it's then I get my best ideas and brain waves as I like to call them. When we are wounded it can become a perverse pleasure so we are inclined to hold on to it. We are afraid if we move into the unknown it is that which frightens us making it difficult to re value negativity and ignore our potential to grow The only effective way to let it become creative is to transform it to the positive. That contributes to who you are, and we are all so different.

Art is a great gift I believe, in dealing with negativity. We all have some gift not one of us are here by accident and we all have a contribution to make to life. Eventually if we look hard enough we do find it.

What our special gift is I believe no one else can perform that job or duty whatever you choose to name it, like you, being as we are all unique. I find this to be true. Marrying young for instance, thrown in the deep end you adjust and learn very quickly and deal with situations and just roll with the punches.

Children are good teachers too, their individuality unknown to yourself you are learning from them. I was so unaware of the responsibility I had; my children trusted me, depended on me, and looked to me for guidance and love. Had I realised the enormity of this I don't believe I could have done it.

MEMORIES AGAIN FLOODING BACK

My sister Margaret, being the domesticated one, enjoyed washing up and cleaning in general, not showing much interest in school. When Daddy would be impressing upon her how important her homework was she would say, "I don't need all that education, when I can do domestic work."

Ironically and sadly Margaret died aged 14, with meningitis. Holding her hand while she was very ill, she told me a nun called to see her and said she was going to Heaven. Margaret replied, "I don't want to go to Heaven, I want to stay with mammy." I was aged twenty myself at this time and with a baby boy.

Recalling I had Noel in my arms and was pregnant with Joseph and found it so distressing while visiting her. She loved Noel, sometimes pushing him in his pram, he was then 16 months old. It was so sad consoling her, knowing she was going to die.

My parents were both with her when she died. I was on my way to visit her, leaving the pram at the bottom of the stone steps of the hospital. Reaching the ward, which was a very long ward with fire lighting at the far end, I noticed Margaret's bed undone with just the mattress.

✳

Instinctively I knew she was gone but I couldn't stop myself walking towards the bed, when a nurse followed me putting her hand on my shoulder and said, "Margaret died at 2:30, your parents were with her, they have not long gone." She then handed me a brown paper parcel containing her clothes.

It was a painful and sad time. My thoughts were with my parents as she was a special sort of girl. They had a lot to remember about her. She loved Saturdays and would take an old pram we had to collect firewood in the summer with her friends in the street. The old pram would rattle along as she pushed her load home.

Margaret's death left a big void in the house for a long time.

DESCRIBING MY CHILDREN

Emotionally we are a very close family.

Joseph I would describe as responsible, intelligent, having a good relationship with the Man above, and appreciates his wife and family.

Mags - Attractive, artistic, generous and popular, with wings on her feet.

Mary - Well she was the solid one, lovely in nature, a very pretty, private person laughed her way through life, yet did not suffer fools gladly and generous to the point of embarrassment.

Billy - Could express himself well, is witty and popular with people, strong minded, clever, a good artist with a sense of duty and does not show his feelings easily.

Annie - Pretty, good natured, speaks her mind, could be moody and sensitive, a caring deposition.

I feel this is a pretty accurate description of my family that emerged from all the turmoil.

Grandchildren and Great grandchildren

Briege, would be the one to shine for looks and personality, a real tonic to meet and chat to, a pain growing up but developed into a very responsible young woman. Married an Irish man and now has 3 beautiful children living in Ireland.

Paula, also married, has 3 children. She is a nurse in the special baby care unit, also a very pretty girl very sensible, sensitive and serious.

Kate, also nursing is a very attractive young lady with a complicated personality. She has not yet found her goal, underestimates herself and would like to travel before settling down.

Deborah, my godchild, I would describe her as very special, unassuming, shy yet very capable. She is also nursing, now married to Shaun he is also of Irish descent. They have 2 children, Anna and Jo Jo.

Jack, a polite handsome boy, bright and likeable undecided about what he wants to do with his life, loves his dog and mostly enjoys his own company.

Aiden, lives in Toronto with his girl friend and baby son.

Steve, lovely humoured, doing quite well, worked his way up in business in consultancy work, a few girl friends on the go I would imagine.

It is very gratifying to see how responsible my grand children's husbands are, sharing responsibilities and above all communicating so well with each other, a very important part of marriage.

EAST MIDLANDS, ENGLAND, 15th MAY 2004

It is a beautiful morning sitting at my living room window, so much to see and admire. The paddock at the back of my garden looks very lush, surrounded by some beautiful chestnut trees coming into full bloom now.

Sounds of the birds singing, two pheasants have passed – so elegant, the horses trotting around, occasionally lifting their heads and biting the leaves from the trees, keeping them perfectly trimmed, often trotting to my fence hoping perhaps I will feed them sugar lumps or carrots.

Our maintenance man, Paul, started cutting our lawns surrounding the bungalows early this morning. Taking him four hours to complete, chatting with some of the tenants as he went cheerfully about his work.

My landlord, David, noticed I was struggling to find somewhere suitable for my bird feeder. On returning from shopping one day I discovered he had put a suitable post up opposite the window where I could watch the tiny birds feed from the peanuts. I hung the feeder from a cup hook which I managed to screw into the side of the post. However, David had a much better idea of placing the feeder on top of the stake securing it with such ease. It amazed me, now I have a perfect post and feeder to watch the birds feed, thanks to David.

17th MAY, 2004 – A BEAUTIFUL WARM DAY

Bill my son-in-law, put up a retractable clothes line for me so it does not take from the beautiful view in my garden. As the summer progresses the view of the paddock and leafy trees, well groomed horses trotting around continually feeding from the grass. The owners come in suitably garbed, ready to go riding, waving to me as they pass my garden.

My cousin, Paul, from Toronto returning from his visit to Ireland called to see me last weekend. We are quite close in age and relate well to each other about the old times and all the hardships of the 30's, 40's and 50's. He was so delighted to see me well settled in such impressive surroundings. Remarking, " I am so happy for you.

It took a long time, but you sure landed on your feet at last."Bringing it home to me all the more, I did in the end seem to make all the right moves, and still have the drive to continue. It's an inner strength that I attribute to my faith in God!

My youngest daughter, Annie, celebrated her 50th birthday yesterday. She is beautiful with lots of blonde hair. Our lives seem to be racing by now. Mags doesn't look her age either, very slim and bubbly, a very thoughtful girl. They were always together, we talk about Mary all the time Life is not the same!

Glancing out the windows as I write, I notice the horses have taken shade from the sun. It's relaxing to watch them, they move so easily.

Actually, I am being very hard on myself today. I love music. I bought a disc especially, because it has Mary's favourite song on it. 'Love changes everything.' It's playing one of my songs now, 'At the Balalalika.'

Although I have done nothing really, it has been an eventful day and my pen is gliding easily across the page as I write from my heart. Maybe it will help me, and although we have no stake in tomorrow, if please God it comes, I will feel better as I often do, and believe I will see Mary again one day, and accept she is at peace forever, where nothing will ever hurt her again!

Like every mother I love all my children, and went through all the hurts of life with them. I am sure I did my best, I hope I did anyway. Reflecting on my own life, now convinced I am very wounded, but not bitter, maybe I loved too much.

Telling a priest at one time, "There is something deep here inside me, I would love to take out and throw away."

Replying, he said," That is the bruise that will never leave you. Your memory keeps reminding you, otherwise you would be an ejit." This put everything into perspective and quite suddenly I understood.

My grand-daughter has three children, and works in a special baby care unit in a local hospital. (It's uncanny her mother works in the delivery room so near, that she can actually hand over the very premature babies to her daughter to keep them alive with her care). On one visit, while chatting about when she was young, and how she used to confide in me, I asked her ,"Are you happy love?"

Replying she said, "Nan I am so happy, it frightens me. He is a wonderful father and husband!"

What a complete contrast to my own life. I was filled with joy for her.

My landlord, not being of the same faith as my self, and while we were both admiring the beautiful display of trees surrounding his properties, I remarked, "Of course, only God can make a tree." Pointing his finger at me jovially saying, "I knew you would say that!" We both ended up laughing.

The birds were chirping away this evening, The tiny ones splashing away in the bird bath as I took in my washing, and rolled back the line.

Wakening up on a beautiful Sunday morning, drawing back the curtains, opening the door onto the patio still in my dressing-gown, the scenery was truly lovely. The trees seemed to spread more and more around the paddock. The horses nudging their heads over the fence so relaxed. Just lovely animals, well looked after and beautifully groomed.

Loathed to leave the tranquillity, I went for my shower. Getting out a pair of trousers, t-shirt, and 'runners.' I was ready for my walk.

It was 9.30a.m. with not many cars on the road to distract me, I was able to concentrate on the expanse of fields to my right as I walked. Lovely houses just peeping behind a thick wooded area of trees on the opposite side of the road, reminding me of Ireland. There is so much beauty everywhere if we take time to look!

Meeting a couple on my walk, as they came towards me, cheerfully saying, "Good morning", took me by surprise. Somehow my memories of years in England, were that people were very private and maybe a bit guarded, not acknowledging you as you passed by. Back home everyone spoke to you, maybe with just a, " Well how are ye? Or, "It's a grand morning thank God!" They seem to have all the time in the world.

Arriving home, making myself a cup of tea, I sat outside on the seat Annie had made in Mary's memory. It takes a special place in my garden, where I often sit and wish she was still beside me. She would love the surroundings, so alive with wild life. But I am sure she is very close, as she assured me she would be.

Pondering also as I sit here, on the people who reached out to help me. A special friend coming to mind in my early years in England, a young man then, I recall he and his wife gave me a three piece suite, and had it delivered to my home in the mid 70's. Ironically by my landlord David. Surprising me again, by calling to welcome me back. His wife is now typing my second book. Such kind people I pray for you all, a big thank you. You can never imagine how much your support and kindness meant to me, through the difficult and, turbulent and eventful years.

CONSOLATION CARD SENT TO ME
AFTER MARY'S DEATH

When I must leave you for a little while
Please do not grieve and shed wild tears
And hug your sorrow to you through the years
But start out bravely with a gallant smile
And for my sake and in my name
Live on and do all things the same
Feed not your loneliness on empty days
But fill each waking hour in useful ways
Reach out your hand to comfort and to cheer
And I in turn will comfort you
And hold you near
And never never be afraid to die
For I am waiting for you in the sky.

2nd December 2004

Epilogue

Brigid looks back at life - remembering the people that brought so much consolation.

Looking back at life with my 80th year fast approaching and not expecting to live to this age, I like myself enough to feel I did well - coped with most situations on my own and I seldom asked advice, knowing people would always be reluctant to give their opinion. Joseph, my eldest son would tactfully tell me what he thought. I valued his opinion, he read a lot and was very intelligent.

I am told I had lots of energy, the remark often being made, "How do you keep going?" I did find it hard to relax. That did not surprise me too much as I suffered with depression and anxiety from the age of 30. I could not let it get me down, there was far too much to do. Being on medication most of the time I knew was only a crutch, but it helped me a lot through my life. I still could laugh and on the bad days I did cry, it was sometimes like a see-saw.

Thinking thank God for the good days and the wonderful people I met through my life, even the doctors who listened sympathetically, not saying much, they didn't have to.

Instinctively I realised they understood and I often drew strength from that.

❋

A special nun always would say something to make me feel good and make me laugh. On one occasion reading some writing I had done, she said, "The thing that strikes me most on reading this, is that you still have your sanity." That actually made me feel very strong, but then of course, trouble does make you stronger.

A Priest on another occasion said, "You are a strong woman, especially up here," pointing to his head.

A lady who counselled me after the death of my lovely daughter, cried with me, and then we would end up laughing, she felt I was very close to God. At the time I didn't feel I was, in fact I thought he was very far away.

I'm told when you feel that it is then he is closest. I often saw God in some people's faces. They didn't have to say much, just a smile, or a hand on your arm. I pick up vibes easily and sense atmospheres quickly.

My daughters are around if I need them. They now have their own families and responsibilities, very capable girls. I still do all my housework and shopping and appreciate a lift with the shopping.

Joseph is now semi-retired with a nice comfortable home and his wife retiring from nursing next year. Billy is more than half way through building his own 4 bedroom house, doing all the work alone except for the roof and managing his money very well.

❋

Also, my friend by the seaside in Ireland, never forgets to pray for me, phones me regularly and sends me two special magazines every month.

Very special people, I wonder what I did to deserve such loyal friends.

Tom is a publisher; he was so interested in my writing, always encouraging me despite being very busy.

Also Ruth Cattell, who was instrumental in amending my manuscript – sending her my appreciation and love.

There was Joan, Sheila, Carmel, so genuine and caring, I will never forget any of you.

My cousins and their wives, I could not even begin to explain their kindness to me during my 13 years in Ireland. Eight families and all of them played a big part in my life, always supporting me and making me welcome. A very unusual family in their generosity and still in touch by phone. I love you all.

Returning to live in England in February, 2004, everything fell into place again for me so easily.

The only drawback was being a bit isolated from the shops and city centre, making me dependent on the family for lifts. Most of the residents have their own transport.

My neighbours are very friendly and the landlord is very helpful, looking in occasionally to see if I'm okay and to have a chat and a laugh, so I am convinced God is very close. These things don't happen by chance.

I hope my book may help women experiencing similar problems in their lives.

With determination and setting yourself a goal, you can come through it without feeling bitter.

If life hands you a lemon, make lemonade!

The tunnel was long but eventually I did see the light.

ISBN 141207779-6